WAGE LABOUR IN DEVELOPING AGRICULTURE

Dedicated to my parents
in the hope that their dedication was not in vain

Wage Labour in Developing Agriculture

Risk, effort and economic development

SUNIL KANWAR
Delhi School of Economics

Ashgate

Aldershot • Brookfield USA • Singapore • Sydney

Published by
Ashgate Publishing Ltd
Gower House
Croft Road
Aldershot
Hants GU11 3HR
England

Ashgate Publishing Company
Old Post Road
Brookfield
Vermont 05036
USA

British Library Cataloguing in Publication Data
Kanwar, Sunil
    Wage labour in developing agriculture : risk, effort and
    economic development
    1.Agriculture - Economic aspects
    I.Title
    331.7'63

Library of Congress Catalog Card Number: 98-71402

ISBN 1 84014 359 2

Printed and bound by Athenaeum Press, Ltd.,
Gateshead, Tyne & Wear.

Contents

List of Figures

List of Tables

Preface

I became interested in rural labour issues during the course of my doctorate at the University of California at Berkeley. The University provided a most invigorating ethos for scholarly work. At the core of this ethos were some of the best faculty one could hope to come across, indeed associate with, anywhere in the world. Not very long after obtaining my doctorate I moved to the Delhi School of Economics. Although things were rather different here, it nevertheless had the reputation of being amongst the best institutions in this part of the world. In this conducive atmosphere I continued exploring issues pertaining to rural labour. This book is the culmination of the last few years of my work in this area.

My initial interest in labour issues was kindled by Pranab Bardhan, George Akerlof and the course on risk and uncertainty that David Zilberman offered at Berkeley. This interest was partially triggered by the widespread concern in the economic development literature about the need for empirical validation of theories and stylized facts which find their way into theoretical models. Especially since it isn't as if there is consensus about the relevance of competing theories and stylization of 'reality'. My reading of the literature revealed this to be particularly true of rural labour-related issues. I further discovered that although a fair bit of theoretical research in this area accounted for the ubiquitous presence of risk in agriculture, the corresponding record in empirical work was very thin if not almost nonexistent. This appeared to point the way for useful research. Jim Chalfant, my principal doctoral supervisor, was instrumental in helping me develop my nascent ideas. His decisiveness and encouraging demeanour are the two qualities that stand out in my mind. I would like to parenthetically add, that in addition to scholarship, observing him (as well as Jeff Perloff and George Akerlof) contributed immensely to my development as an instructor. But over the long run, the one individual who has been the most supportive and responsive is Peter Berck. His good humour and pragmatism were always a welcome foil to the pressures of work. These qualities were amply reflected in his exhortation that I '... should learn to write like the Brooklyn Gangster'. I hope I haven't failed him, at least in spirit. Pranab Bardhan with his sagacity and a myriad interests was always a source of inspiration.

The availability of a 'good quality' data set is central to rigorous and reliable empirical research. For if there are too many question marks on the quality of the data set, and/or the data set is silent on many of the very aspects that you need to consider, no amount of clever theoretical modelling will compensate. Further, the usefulness of the conclusions emanating from enquiries using such data sets would be correspondingly limited. Of course, ultimately no data set is 'complete', and my observations hold only in a relative sense. I was introduced to a rather comprehensive and meticulously compiled data set collected by the International Crops Research Institute for the Semi-Arid Tropics (ICRISAT), by Shankar Subramaniam. Shankar was also to prove a most effective troubleshooter, subsequently, on many occasions. I spent a month at ICRISAT (Hyderabad, India) in the summer of 1990, and had the occasion to visit one of the mandate villages myself. Tom Walker, the then principal economist at ICRISAT, graciously provided me the data tapes. (The Government of India which has perfected the art of sitting tight on data collected with public money, presumably in the public interest, could learn something from this). I also spent numerous fruitful hours in discussion with him. His first hand knowledge of the Indian rural scene was impressive, given his American background. Of course, I do not speak for him or his organisation.

I benefited considerably from seminars at Tilburg University, Institute of Economic Growth, Indian Statistical Institute (Delhi), Vanderbilt University and the Delhi School of Economics. The discussions usually helped, and often forced, me to clarify the issues before me, and hone my arguments. Even outside the seminar halls, I was fortunate to benefit from various individuals by way of discussion or advice at various stages of my research. A partial list of such individuals would include Alain de Janvry, Larry Karp, Betty Sadoulet, Joe Callahan, James Foster, Clive Bell, Kathryn Anderson, K.L. Krishna, Suresh Tendulkar, Santosh Panda, Bharat Ramaswamy, Malashri Lal, and Shalini Shah. Bina Agarwal, Kanchan Chopra, and Peter Berck were kind enough to provide me with comments on various chapters. K. Sundaram and Ranen Das also went through some of the material included here and obliged me with their criticisms. I would also like to mention a special word of gratitude for Kaushik Basu who was never grudging with his time or encouraging words.

Another crucial ingredient in such an enterprise is infrastructural support. My experience in the different institutions that I have been associated with over the course of this work has been, to put it mildly, somewhat uneven. In the U.S. the excellent logistical support made my task that much easier. The efficiency of Gail, Sherry, Bessie, Louise and Mouzon Siddiqui, and their ever-smiling faces made even mundane dealings pleasurable. The knowledgable Grace was an asset in the library. The patience and promptness with which Jim Bradley, Sam Scalise and Gary Casterline helped me was remarkable. In the Delhi School of Economics the infrastructure has become quite tolerable in the last couple of years. I appreciate the willing help rendered by Kamal Sharma, Nazma Sultana, Mr. Ramachandran, Muthu and Vinayan, that marked a departure from the status quo ante.

Finally, my family was an important factor in helping me accomplish this goal, especially my little son Susheem who I would eagerly look forward to meeting at the end of a hard day's labour.

Sunil Kanwar
Delhi School of Economics

1 Motivating the Major Issues

Introduction

John Dos Passos, in *Century's Ebb*, chronicled rather evocatively that 'Haying seemed to attract thunderstorms. Great purple and yellow and white cauliflower clouds would start making up in the western sky. The boys would pitch and pitch until they were ready to drop ... It was a race. The last one in was a rotten egg'. Of course, untimely thunderstorms are hardly the only phenomena that imperil cultivation. And the 'last one in' is often worse than a rotten egg — he is likely to go belly up. That farmers have always had to make decisions under various conceivable uncertain or risky conditions would be stating the obvious. The production process is extremely susceptible to the caprices of the weather. The paucity of rainfall, or else its superabundance, its lack of proper correspondence with the various stages of production, blight, frost, pestilence, and other such factors contribute greatly to an uncertain yield. Further, the product prices that farmers face may be quite different at the end of the cropping season than they were at the time the sowing decisions were initially made. Therefore, the need to incorporate risk into the different aspects of agricultural decision-making has been recognised as virtually imperative. Indeed, Newbery and Stiglitz (1981, p. 8) observe that '... agricultural economists were among the first economists to realize the importance of risk to an understanding of the functioning of the economy ...'. Nevertheless, the explicit incorporation of risk into the empirical analyses of various rural issues has been conspicuous by its neglect. Most of the earlier empirical studies concerning rural decision-making are couched in a certainty framework and hence ignore the importance of risk. It is important to recognize, however, the deleterious impact that risk might have on incomes and consumption, especially in environments where the buffer against such negative influences is thin at best. While the short run effects of risk may be malnutrition, morbidity and poverty, in the long run it may well be mortality. Accepting the undesirableness of such consequences both in the micro and the macro, it becomes important to study the influence of risk vis-à-vis the various aspects of farm decision-making, and consider if policy can ameliorate the situation somewhat. An added impetus in this direction is provided by the fact that the predominant proportion of developing country populations reside in rural areas even today, that this proportion has undergone a rather slow decline in many countries, and that in some south Asian countries it has hardly declined at all.

Issues Concerning the Market Supply of Labour

One area of significant interest is that of farmers' off-farm labour allocation decisions. Since farmers, by definition, have self-cultivation as their primary occupation, they are directly exposed to the numerous production risks. Ignoring issues such as the staggered use of (some) inputs over the production cycle, and given that input prices are known at the time the input-use decisions are undertaken, we may assume away cost uncertainty. Experience shows that this is the least important form of production risk, so that our assumption is probably fairly plausible. Therefore, we shall focus our attention on yield risk or rather, given the need to aggregate over multiple outputs, on revenue risk. Since crop production spans the production period, it is susceptible to risks at different points of time over this period. For instance the pre-sowing rains might play truant, particularly in the semi-arid regions, jeopardizing the sowing of staple crops. Further, sub-optimal pre-sowing rains and a poor distribution of rain over the production period may adversely affect the prospects of the crops grown, potentially lessening the labour required for intermediate operations such as weeding, mulching, fertilising etc., as also for harvesting and threshing at the end of the production period. Of course, these deleterious effects of the production risks become manifest only as the crops mature, and particularly at harvest time. But in an effort to hedge these risks before they have worked themselves out, farm households may try to switch out of self-cultivation and find work — farm-related or nonfarm — in the local casual labour market (see Figure 1.1).[1]

It is a well-known fact of developing agriculture, that the predominant bulk of farm households are small cultivators, and therefore their resource base proves insufficient to gainfully employ them the year round even when production conditions are normal. Consequently, they fall back on the daily casual labour market whenever possible, such that off-farm labour income is often a fairly substantial contributor to total income. Given the

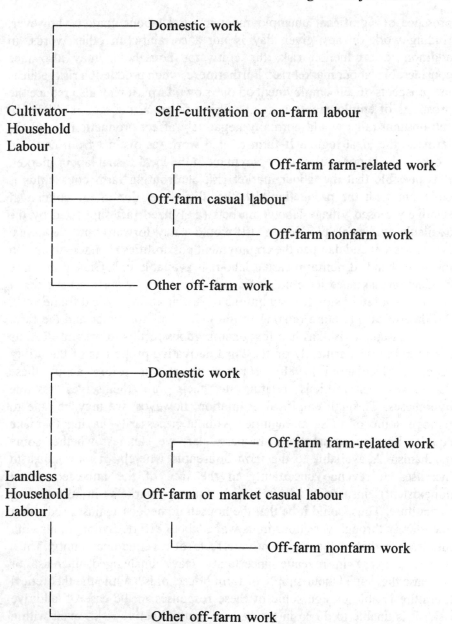

Figure 1.1 Allocation of family labour time by cultivator and landless households

presence of significant unemployment in rural labour markets, however, finding work on any given day is not a certainty. In other words, in addition to production risk, the cultivator households may also face considerable labour market risk. Furthermore, when production risk reduces the prospects of self-employment on one's own farm, it may also reduce the prospects of employment on neighbouring farms in the region. After all, sub-optimal rains would normally negatively affect production on all the farms in the local region. If farm-related work (as distinct from nonfarm work) is the major source of employment in the local casual labour market, it is possible that the labour market risk confronting farm households is covariant with the production risk that they face. For in the context of relatively closed village labour markets (a stylized fact supported by the available evidence), production risk would 'carry forward' into the casual labour market and dampen the employment possibilities available there. On the other hand, if nonfarm casual labour is available in sufficient measure production risk need have no significant impact on labour market risk.

Despite rather simple assumptions regarding the analytical framework, the theoretical literature relating to the individual consumer and the farm household under risk has had few unambiguous results to present. Results are found to turn critically on the third derivative properties of the utility function (Dardanoni, 1988). Having no strong priors about these derivatives, assumptions relating to them are themselves testable hypotheses. Through empirical estimation, however, we may be able to remove some of these ambiguities without necessarily having to make equally limiting assumptions. In particular, we can test whether some mechanism is available to the farm household whereby it may adjust to increases in revenue uncertainty in the face of the imperfect (even nonexistent) insurance, capital and futures markets in developing agriculture. Thus, could it be that the household hedges against production uncertainty through variations in its wage labour effort? Synonymous with this issue is that of the 'disincentive effects' of revenue uncertainty. Thus, will a decrease in revenue uncertainty leave unchanged, increase or decrease the wage labour supply of farm households? While the theoretical literature is able to sign some of these responses in the case of 'additive risk', it is unable to do so in the case of 'multiplicative risk'[2] even within the framework of rather simple models (see Block and Heineke, 1973; Dardanoni, *ibid.*). When the model framework is expanded to allow for endogenous income and a multiple argument utility function (as in the case of a farm household model, for instance), even the additive risk results may become open to question. Moreover, apart from making the analysis conceptually weaker, ignoring risk factors would also lead to a specification bias.

Closely intertwined with these issues is that of the implications of the price stabilisation schemes for agricultural commodities. Hitherto, the impact of price stabilisation policies has been analysed in terms of efficiency gains and changes in producer revenues from on-farm production (Newbery and Stiglitz, *ibid.*). But given that primary producers may also supply significant amounts of off-farm labour, as we noted above for developing country farmers, stabilisation policies may have a significant impact on their market labour income as well. And it is possible that this latter effect may overwhelm those on efficiency gains and revenues from self-cultivation. The implications of our study on these broader aspects of price stabilisation policies shall, however, be somewhat incidental. For although we point out the potential importance of this issue, we do not pursue it in any detail in this monograph.

Finally, there remains the question whether inclusion of risk variables in the analyses of off-farm labour supply, will alter quantitatively and/or qualitatively the effects of the other explanatory variables on the hiring out of labour by farm households. It would be interesting, particularly, to note the off-farm labour supply response with respect to the wage rate in the specific Indian context. Of the earlier studies, Bardhan (1979a) finds a significantly negative wage response for his sample of cultivators in rural India. Rosenzweig (1980) reports a similar result for male labour, using another sample of Indian farm households. Considering the predominant proportion of males in the total labour force, Rosenzweig's result leads us to expect a similar inverse association between total (i.e. male plus female) off-farm labour supply and the wage rate. In view of the near subsistence conditions of the bulk of the labour supplying farmers, we find these results to be somewhat disconcerting. Could it be that the omission of the risk variables biased the wage response of off-farm labour supply by an amount large enough to change its sign?

Issues Concerning the Demand for Labour

Another significant area in which the received empirical literature does not consider the influence of risk, is the demand for hired labour. In fact, studies on the demand for hired labour *per se* are rather scanty. Considering that production risk directly affects the self-cultivation activities of farmers, it stands to reason that it may significantly affect their demand for labour, both family as well as hired. Furthermore, if we allow for the fact that farmers are even today the major providers of employment in the rural setup, avenues of nonfarm wage employment still being relatively few at least in south Asia, the influence of risk on the hiring-in of labour may have significant consequences for rural households. Indeed, the importance of risk factors may have increased over time, what with the green revolution being associated not only with increasing expected returns from production, but also with an increasing variance of returns. In a model of the demand for labour under risk, therefore, some of the older questions become relevant anew. What are the important shifter variables of the demand for hired labour curve? In the context of a positive price policy being the cornerstone of agricultural policies in many developing (as also developed) countries, are the price factors or the nonprice (specifically, risk) factors, relatively important shifter variables? With respect to the risk factors, there is the further question whether they shift the demand for hired labour curve inwards or outwards. The theoretical literature on input demand under risk (Batra and Ullah, 1974; Sandmo, 1971; Horowitz, 1970) shows that a marginal increase in production risk will cause a *decline* in the demand for labour (given decreasing absolute risk aversion and a 'well behaved' production function). If this negative effect were statistically strong and associated with a high enough elasticity, a positive price policy that is associated with an increasing variance of net returns may well prove inefficacious in raising the demand for labour.

Other Major Considerations

Production and labour market risks become all the more pronounced in semi-arid regions, and may therefore be presumed to be relatively important explanatory factors in the economies of these regions. By the same token, their omission from the empirical investigation of the problems of these areas is likely to be that much more serious. Semi-arid agriculture constitutes a very large proportion of agriculture in less developed economies even today, whether we measure this in terms of area cultivated, magnitude of foodgrains production, or simply the number of households whose livelihood and welfare it directly affects. Despite this, it has been relatively neglected and is characterised by poor infrastructure, low investment, high risks and abject poverty. It would be trite to say that the semi-arid tracts have largely missed out on the green revolution. So also have these regions been neglected as regards research into various aspects of agriculture-based economic development, with the focus of interest having been the dynamic, irrigated tracts. This study aims to redress this imbalance in a small way.

We feel that farm household decision-making should be studied within a farm household production framework. Since farmers are both consumers and producers of their staples, the representative consumer model implicitly or explicitly employed by some of the earlier studies analysing the market supply of labour would, in other words, be inappropriate. Its use may yield seriously biased results, and this bias may be significant (see Singh, Squire and Strauss, 1986, for evidence).

The use of farm household models would require detailed farm-household data, which are available to us in the form of a unique cross section-time series. Data sets employed by the earlier empirical studies were usually cross-sections rather than cross section-time series in nature. Moreover, they were usually not detailed enough, even though their coverage may have been very wide. Thus, although the National Sample Surveys for India (used by Bardhan, 1979a, 1984a, 1984b) report data for several thousand rural households, these data pertain to a single cross-section and do not provide information on a large number of relevant variables. This is graphically expressed by Bardhan (1984a, p. 7) who writes that '[I]n the econometric exercises ... I did not have requisite data on some of the obviously important variables; for some others ... I had to make do with proxy variables. In some other cases ... the level of aggregation was not right ... '. While it is often not possible to do much about many of these problems, at the same time one cannot escape the fact that they could lead to serious specification bias in the empirical results obtained (despite the brilliance otherwise of these studies). For the same reason, inferences and recommendations for policy based on such empirical evidence would be suspect, and, at the very least, would need to be supplemented with more information.

Significant unemployment, we observed above, was a stylized fact of rural labour markets in developing agriculture. On the other hand, there may be periods in the agricultural cycle, such as sowing and harvest times, when the demand for timely labour may exceed its supply. In both situations, the short side of the market is likely to be of relative importance, that is, labour demand in situations of excess supply and labour supply in situations of excess demand. Taking the agricultural cycle as a whole, at the very least this seems to imply that a supply-demand simultaneous equations framework may be more relevant than one focusing on the supply and demand sides of the labour market alone. But, further, the existence of unemployment makes the estimation of *equilibrium* supply-demand models inappropriate. More pertinent, therefore, would be the formulation and estimation of an appropriate *disequilibrium* model of the labour market — namely, one that takes account of the excess supply or excess demand in each of the years of the sample period. This study is an attempt to extend the extant literature in all the above-mentioned dimensions.

Overview

Chapter 2 commences with a review of the received literature on off-farm labour supply. The preponderant proportion of this research deals with the issue of agricultural labour supply without acknowledging the presence of risk as potentially pertinent or empirically important to farm household decision-making. Even though a small part of the previous research does attempt to model the influence of risk, we find that it does so rather inadequately and falls short of taking up the issues that we are interested in. When analysing the supply of labour, due allowance should be made for the fact that the economic units at the source of this supply are not homogeneous. Very broadly, we may classify the labour market as consisting of two categories of workers — the landless labourers, and the self-employed or (mostly small) cultivators. In general, we cannot assume the labour supply response of *either category* to represent the *aggregate* labour supply response. This is particularly true of underdeveloped agriculture, which has been traditionally characterised by a very large proportion of farm households operating in the casual labour market. Their meagre and impoverished resource base proves insufficient to fully employ the available family labour, so that a significant proportion of these households supply their labour for off-farm work and account for a large proportion of the total labour supplied in the casual labour market. As a consequence, in addition to the labour-leisure choice which the labourers have to make, the cultivators must also make a choice between labour supply for self-cultivation and off-farm or market labour supply. With a view to facilitating a discussion of the relevant issues, therefore, we construct a decision-theoretic household production model under risk for the cultivator households. Alternative assumptions about the prevalent 'risk regime' — 'additive' or 'multiplicative' — lead us to alternative estimable models of labour supply and demand. Discussion of labour supply issues would not be complete, however, without a consideration of the landless or agricultural labour households. This chapter closes, therefore, with a brief discussion of the labour supply model appropriate for landless households.

The data set used for the empirical analysis is discussed in chapter 3. The availability of a detailed cross section-time series pertaining to a fairly large number of household units makes for a unique and powerful data set. These data were collected by the International Crops Research Institute for the Semi-Arid Tropics (ICRISAT), as part of their village level surveys. The sample design is such as to make the sample villages representative of their respective semi-arid zones, so that the empirical results obtained may be taken to be fairly generally valid for the Indian semi-arid regions as a whole. A rough sketch of the sample units is provided by the mean levels of statistics characterising them. This serves to establish the poor resource base — physical as well as human capital — of the sample households, and the high risks confronting them. The chapter goes on to discuss the derivation of the risk variables, and the conceptual and measurement problems associated with such an exercise. It concludes with a discussion of the computation of the wage rate variable as used in this study.

As we had mentioned earlier, it is quite possible that the production and labour market risks are covariant in the context of relatively closed village level labour markets. Chapter 4 discusses this possibility and attempts to empirically test for such causation. After considering the stationarity properties of the variables representing production and labour market risks, empirical tests of causality between these variables are conducted. The tests are first conducted at the aggregate level, and then confirmed for the disaggregated data, where the disaggregation is done both by village and by gender. The implications of the results for the farm household production model under risk are then considered.

Chapter 5 commences with a discussion of the need for estimating the demand for labour under risk, with our specific interest being the demand for *hired* labour. A thorough discussion of the exogenous variables of interest is first presented. This complements the derivation of the estimating demand model outlined in chapter 2, where the exogenous variables were mentioned but not discussed in any detail in order to keep the derivation of the estimating model uncluttered. This is followed by a discussion of the estimation results and their policy implications.

Chapter 6 begins by considering the issues involved in estimating the alternative models of off-farm labour supply that were derived in chapter 2. The specification of the economic models is completed with a detailed discussion of the factors exogenous to, and potentially important for, the regressand. Again, this complements the theoretical derivation of the labour supply models presented in chapter 2. A discussion explaining and justifying the particular estimation method adopted is also presented. Estimation exercises are then carried out for total household labour supplied by both the cultivator households as well as landless households. Within the former category, the off-farm labour supply of women is further analysed. This is followed by an analysis of wage functions for the different groups of labour suppliers considered above, and the implications these results might have for the alternative theories of rural wage determination. The chapter concludes by supplementing the partial analyses of the supply and demand sides of the casual labour market, with the analysis of a *disequilibrium* simultaneous equations system of supply and demand.

Finally, chapter 7 presents a brief summary and some further interpretations of the estimation results discussed in the previous chapters. The results obtained in our study are compared with those from several other developing countries in order to place them in proper perspective.

Notes

1   Off-farm labour may be supplied either in the daily casual labour market or in 'other off-farm work' such as tied labour. Tied labour, however, accounts for a very small proportion of the market labour supplied (more detail in subsequent chapters). Moreover, a tied labourer is bound by a 'long term' contract to his employer, whereas a daily casual labourer can alternate between working on his own farm and working off-farm (in the casual labour market). Therefore, we focus on off-farm work in the daily casual labour market.

2   Additive and multiplicative risks are defined in chapter 2 below.

2 Decision-Theoretic Models of Farm Behaviour

Introduction

Sherlock Holmes, in *A Study in Scarlet*, remarked somewhat admonishingly to his companion Dr. Watson, that 'It is a capital mistake to theorize before you have ... the evidence. It biases the judgement'. While controversial, this opinion is not entirely wrong either. Unfortunately, the early development theorists did not quite listen. Although several generations of models of economic development were premised on a variety of assumptions about the mode of agricultural or rural labour supply response to various economic and noneconomic factors, there was little hard evidence to support or disprove these labour supply theories till recently. The pioneering work of Bardhan (1979a), Barnum and Squire (1979) and Lau *et.al.* (1978) went some way in improving our understanding of rural labour supply behaviour, and paved the way for substantial research in this area. But even though a host of empirical studies concerning these issues are now available, the bulk of this research ignores the impact of production risks on market labour supply behaviour. This may be a serious omission, however, as we argued in the previous chapter. In the recent past, though, some authors *have* attempted to consider the impact of risk on farmers' labour supply decisions. But they do not quite achieve their objective. From a critique of these studies emerges the justification for our present research. In reviewing the past literature we take trouble in pointing out not just the omission of risk variables, but various other shortcomings as well which need to be taken careful account of in conducting an empirical study of labour supply behaviour. To this end, we develop a decision-theoretic household model for cultivators in the context of risky agriculture. The model results are found to turn on the particular assumptions we make about the risk attitudes of the farmers in question, and the manner in which risk is incorporated into the model structure. As regards the former, the burden of evidence points towards risk aversion on the part of cultivators. This leaves us with the task of specifying an appropriate risk regime. Not having any strong priors as to what this should

11

be, we develop estimable models based on alternative specifications of the risk regime. *A priori*, one may justifiably expect the results to differ under the alternative specifications. Although the primary focus of this chapter is on the development of the labour supply relation for *cultivator* households, the concluding section considers the labour supply relation for landless households, since this is the other major group participating in rural labour markets. We begin with a critique of the earlier studies.

Antecedents — Models without Risk

In one of the earliest studies of labour supply in Indian agriculture, Bardhan (1979a) estimated labour supply functions using cross-section household data from rural West Bengal. He found that though the wage response was significantly positive for landless labourers (Bardhan's equation 1), and landless labourers and small cultivators[1] taken together (Bardhan's equation 2), it was significantly *negative* for cultivators[2] *per se* (Bardhan's equation 5). Even when positive, the elasticity of labour supply was small at around 0.2 to 0.3. These results partially substantiate the point we made above, that landless and cultivator households are not homogeneous categories, so that the labour supply response of neither category should be presumed representative of the overall labour supply response.[3] A simple clubbing together of the two groups may not, therefore, be quite appropriate. Bardhan goes on to observe that '... labour supply is primarily determined by other economic, social, and demographic constraints ...' (p. 81). Thus, he finds hiring out behaviour to be consistently negatively related to plot size and the educational level of adults in the family. With regard to the latter result, note that Bardhan considered off-farm *farm-related work* only, and not off-farm work in all activities, i.e. farm as well as nonfarm. He argued that a relatively educated person may find it unpalatable to work on someone else's farm. leading us to expect an inverse relationship between off-farm work and education. We feel, however, that the relevant variable should be total off-farm work in the daily, casual labour market, and not off-farm farm-related work only. If the possibility of off-farm *nonfarm* work were allowed for, the association between off-farm work and education may go either way.

Lau *et.al.* (1978), Barnum and Squire (1979), Adulavidhaya *et.al.* (1984), Singh and Janakiram (1986) and Strauss (1986) all used various parameterisations of a farm household model to study labour supply in Taiwan, Malaysia, Thailand, Korea and Nigeria, and Sierra Leone, respectively. They found small but positive wage-elasticities of labour supply ranging between 0.1 and 0.3. A problem with complete parameterisation of a framework may be the implausible assumptions which that entails. For instance, use of the linear logarithmic expenditure system to model the consumption side of household models implies that the expenditure elasticities with respect to total income equal unity. Again, the linear expenditure system is based on the additivity assumption, which may be too restrictive (Deaton and Muellbauer, 1980). In Adulavidhaya *et.al. different samples of farmers* were used for estimating the consumption and production sides of the model! Further, barring one sample of Sierra Leone farmers, all other estimates relate to *total* labour supply, i.e. labour supply on one's own farm plus off-farm labour supply. This still leaves us in the dark regarding *off-farm* or market labour supply responses. Even the Sierra Leone estimates must be discounted in view of the somewhat implausible results. Thus, the off-farm labour supply elasticity is reported as 17.2!.

Huffman (1980) analysed the off-farm labour supply decisions of a sample of American farmers. The operators' wage response turned out to be significantly positive with an elasticity of about 0.3, for both the 'proportion participating' as well as the 'number of off-farm work days'. Education had a significantly positive effect on off-farm labour supply, in contrast to Bardhan's finding; although we should not lose sight of the developing country context of Bardhan's study as opposed to the developed country context of Huffman's study. Moreover, as Sumner (1982) argues, given the Cobb-Douglas form of Huffman's production function, a ceteris paribus increase in schooling will imply a *reduction* in off-farm labour supply;[4] so that Huffman's empirical result contradicts the implication of his theoretical model. A significant weakness of Huffman's study is that he uses *county averages per farm* and not household data to estimate his *farm household* model.

Rosenzweig (1980) estimates a household production model for a 1970-71 cross-section of Indian farmers. He finds the *net* labour supply curve for cultivator household males to be backward bending, the wage elasticity of off-farm labour days being about -0.2. The male education variable is significantly negatively related with male off-farm labour supply; which, he explains, implies that schooling improves their on-farm marginal value productivity. The wives' education seems to enhance this relationship. The age variables, husbands or wives', are not significant although they have the right signs. Thus, the quadratic, life-cycle relation discovered in other studies is not corroborated. The coefficients for exogenous income, cultivated area and irrigation have the expected negative signs and are significant. The equation for females displays much the same results, except that the wage response is positive and significant. Rosenzweig's results, however, cannot be taken at face value. To see this, let the net labour supply function that he estimates be:

$$NL^s = \alpha + \beta \, x \tag{2.1}$$

where NL^s is *net* labour supply and x is some relevant regressor(s). Let the labour supply and labour demand relations underlying the above relation be:

$$L^s = \alpha_0 + \beta_0 \, x \tag{2.2}$$

$$L^d = \alpha_1 + \beta_1 \, x \tag{2.3}$$

where L^s is labour supply and L^d is labour demand such that $NL^s = L^s - L^d$, $\beta_1 < 0$, and either $\beta_0 < 0$ or $\beta_0 > 0$. From this it trivially follows that when $\beta < 0$ we have:

$$\beta = \beta_0 - \beta_1 < 0 \text{ iff } \beta_0 < 0 \text{ } and \text{ } |\beta_0| > |\beta_1|$$

In other words, only if the above condition holds will a backward-bending relation of *net* labour supply (NL^s) with respect to some regressor x imply a backward-bending relation of labour supply *per se* (L^s) with respect to that x. If, however, $|\beta_0| < |\beta_1|$, a backward-bending *net* labour supply relation will not imply a backward-bending labour supply relation. Further, when $\beta > 0$ we may have:

$$\beta_0 < 0 \text{ } and \text{ } |\beta_0| < |\beta_1|$$

In other words, when *net* labour supply is upward-sloping with respect to some x, that does not necessarily imply that labour supply *per se* is also upward-sloping with respect to that x. The implication of these proofs is, that Rosenzweig's results using *net* labour supply as the regressand may not necessarily hold with relation to labour supply *per se*.

Sumner (1982) estimates a static, household production model for a sample of American farmers, and finds that the labour supply response exhibits a quadratic age pattern, and is significantly negatively related to farm experience and training. Two points are worth noting. First, the education variable has a positive, although insignificant, coefficient. Sumner interprets this to mean that '... schooling and farm operator labour are slight substitutes or are independent over at least some ranges of hours'. Secondly, the wage elasticity of off-farm hours supplied *exceeds one*. This contrasts with the earlier results which reported very small wage elasticities. A drawback of this study is, that in the 'participation equations' Sumner does not include the wage rate as a regressor. Nor does he clarify whether this variable was included but found to be insignificant, or else was not included at all for some reason.

Skoufias (1993) analyses the intrafamily allocation of time between the market, home, leisure and schooling activities on the part of an Indian sample of adult males, adult females and children. He finds that male wage labour supply is negatively but insignificantly related to the male wage rate, but female wage labour supply is positively and significantly related to the female wage rate. A problem with his otherwise elegant analysis appears to be that while his labour supply functions contain both personal and household variables, they do not contain any production side variables; so that the functions estimated may be subject to specification bias.

All the studies that we reviewed above were couched in a certainty framework. Some of the recent research in this area, however, does allow for the influence of risk on farmers' labour supply decisions. To gauge the extent to which it has been successful in this objective, we now look at these studies in some detail.

Antecedents — Models with Risk

Parliament (1984) analysed the supply of labour on an Israeli kibbutz or agricultural production cooperative. Several points are noteworthy regarding her analysis. First, she postulates a single argument utility function. This amounts to assuming away all the interesting possibilities of substitution and complementarity that one may wish to consider in the context of labour supply. To wit, the labour-leisure choice and the choice between work on the farm and work off-farm confronting the members of the farm household. Secondly, the empirical part of her research does not really put to test the propositions which she develops in the earlier, theoretical portion. In fact, one might say that the economic models underlying the two sections of her dissertation are themselves dissimilar. In the theoretical section, members are assumed to allocate their time between private and cooperative production so as to maximise the expected utility of uncertain income. She then considers comparative-static changes in: (i) the 'cohesion conjecture' which measures the cohesion or emulation on the part of other members to a change in the labour supply of the member in question, (ii) the proportion of cooperative income distributed, (iii) the correlation between private and cooperative income, and (iv) cooperative income variability. She finds that none of these changes lead to an unambiguous increase in the members' cooperative labour supply. In her empirical analysis, on the other hand, the cooperative income is shared equally between the members and there is no private production. Consequently, as she is quick to admit, it is not possible to determine the effect of changes in parameters such as the income distribution rule, correlation between private and cooperative income, and cooperative income variability, on the supply of labour. Thus, the model she estimates is quite different from the one she develops in the theoretical portion of her study. Furthermore, the estimated model also fails to include the members' risk attitudes, which are measured by the coefficient of absolute risk aversion in the theoretical model. In other words, the estimated model contains no variables pertaining to the uncertainties prevalent in the cooperatives' operating environment; and could have been derived by a simple, *deterministic* utility-maximising exercise.

Roe and Graham-Tomasi (1986) incorporate yield risk into a dynamic version of the agricultural household model. The general model being too complicated, they '... focus on a specific functional form of the general model ...' so that '... unambiguous results can be obtained ...' (p. 263). These are obtained via simulation experiments. For instance, letting yield variance be ±25% of what it is in the 'base solution', they find that the demand for labour declines while the supply of labour increases. Thus, in an attempt to reduce the disutility from '... a higher yield (and hence income) variance ...', the household decreases the scale of activity in the home produced good. It is important that their empirical example of the effect of an increase in risk not be confused with an outright empirical test. As they point out, given the complexity and tedium of working with a full-blown dynamic model, they resort to several simplifications and assumptions as to functional form, in order to present unambiguous results. In so doing, while they employ some statistics relating to the Dominican Republic, *they assume others* such as the parameters of the utility and production functions (see p. 267). Further, if their equations were actually estimated the results would most surely be biased, for the labour supply equation in their model contains only the price and risk variables. Surely, labour supply depends on other important factors as well. In fact, for some labour groups (rural women in India, for instance), some researchers feel that nonprice, caste factors may well be the dominant explanatory factors.[5] Lastly, simulation experiments merely provide us with the percentage change in the 'left hand side' variable for given percentage changes in the 'right hand side' variables, *contingent on the assumed parameter values*. This does not establish, however, whether the changes in the two sets of variables bear a statistically significant relationship to each other.

Fafchamps (1989, 1993) estimates a two-period, nonseparable household production model under risk, for a sample of farmers in the African semi-arid tropics. He conducts several simulation experiments, and finds that while the direct elasticity of substitution in production between period 1 and period 2 labour supply is around 0.5, that for leisure in period 1 vis-a-vis leisure in period 2 is around 3.5-4.0. Fafchamps concludes that '... with values of the elasticity of substitution that high, the household labour supply becomes extremely sensitive to minute changes in the wage ... between periods, too sensitive to make sense'. This result is clearly out of line with those from other studies, which have tended to yield very small elasticities. He opines that possibly the model is unable to distinguish between substitutability in production and substitutability in consumption. With regard to the impact of changes in risk on labour supply, the simulation experiments reveal that the households tend to *increase* their effort when the random shocks are positive, and vice versa. While these results are illuminating, we must not forget that they pertain to *own-farm* labour supply or family labour only. For Fafchamps observes, that for most of the agricultural season *there does not exist a market for hired labour* (so that the households must rely almost totally on their own labour resources). What we are interested in, however, is the effect of risk on the *off-farm* supply of labour.

To recapitulate, in the above section we considered several studies which allowed for the presence of risk in farm household decision-making, in addition to several others in the previous section which did not. We find, however, that all of the studies fall short of meeting the objectives of the present research. Therefore, we feel that ample motivation and justification exist for exploring the empirical relationship between production risk and the off-farm labour supply of farmers.

Decision-Theoretic Household Model

In the previous chapter we argued that the framework of analysis should be suited to the particular labour group that one is interested in studying. This led us to aver, that given our interest in cultivators' off-farm labour supply, the appropriate framework would be the farm household production model. Accordingly, in the following sections we develop a simple household production model under risk and use it to derive various estimable relationships. The standard, static household production model is well expounded in the literature. The household (head) is assumed to maximise a utility function:

$$U = U(a, m, l; Z_1) \qquad U_i > 0, \, U_{ii} < 0; \quad i = a, m, l \qquad (2.4)$$

where a is the consumption of the agricultural staple, m is the consumption of the (composite) market purchased good, l is the consumption of leisure time, and Z_l is the vector of household characteristics. These may include household composition variables such as family size, and the age and sex composition of the household (that is, the number of prime age males, number of prime age females, number of dependent males and number of dependent females). The household's caste status may also be included. We shall discuss these exogenous variables in detail later.

Expenditure on the market purchased good is constrained by (and, in equilibrium, equals) the household's total income (comprising profits, wages and exogenous income),

$$p_m \, m = p_a \, (Q - a) - wL^h + wF_2 + I \qquad (2.5)$$

where p_a is the exogenous price of a, p_m is the exogenous price of m, w is the exogenous nominal wage rate, Q is the household production of the staple, L^h is hired labour, F_2 is off-farm labour supply and I is exogenous income. Given the possibility of unemployment in the labour market, off-farm employment may not be certain. Off-farm labour supply F_2 is then the actual labour supply by the household members *after* this labour market uncertainty has worked itself out.[6]

It would be trite to assert that the farm production process is susceptible to all kinds of risks. What these risks are, we have already specified in chapter 1. We could represent these risks either by (the moments of) an 'additive term' or a 'multiplicative term' in the production function. Although it is debatable whether risk should be included additively or multiplicatively *a priori*, there are compelling reasons to follow the latter specification. These reasons are discussed below where their import is likely to come across more clearly. For the present we just proceed with a multiplicative specification. At the same time, we prefer not to use the Just-Pope multiplicative form (Just and Pope, 1978), for it can be shown that their production function yields a *negative* marginal product for finite output (Fabella, 1989). We therefore model the production function for the household staple as:

$$Q = g(L; Z_2)\epsilon = g(L^h + F_1 ; Z_2) \, \epsilon \qquad g_j > 0, \, g_{jj} < 0; \, j = L^h, F_1 \quad (2.6)$$

where F_1 is on-farm labour supply, ϵ represents multiplicative yield risk such that $E(\epsilon) = \bar{\epsilon}$ and $V(\epsilon) = \sigma^2$. and Z_2 represents the exogenous variables. These may include fixed factors such as land and nonland assets, as well as other factors that affect the productivity of production activities such as the age and education of the household head. The use of other variable inputs is subsumed in this analysis. All these exogenous variables are discussed in detail later when we get down to empirical estimation (chapters 5 and 6). Although we have introduced Z_1 and Z_2 through the utility and production functions, respectively, such a strict dichotomy is neither desirable nor always possible. In the case of some variables it may be possible to argue *a priori* that the variables in question enter both the utility and production functions. Therefore, when we hypothesize the influence of a particular variable in the context of a particular function, this should be viewed more in terms of pedagogic convenience than as a statement of the fact that that is the only way in which that particular variable may enter the system.

It could happen that the labour market risk that we mentioned above may be correlated with the production risk, since we are talking in the context of the local daily rated labour market. For the moment, however, we ignore this possible interdependence, or rather, ignore the possibility of its being statistically significant. We take up this issue in detail in chapter 4. This assumption allows us to keep the theoretical model relatively simple.

Finally, the time constraint facing the household is:

$$1 + F_1 + F_2 = T \qquad\qquad (2.7)$$

where T is the total time available to the household. Substituting equations (2.5), (2.6) and (2.7) into equation (2.4), and assuming that the household (head) maximises expected utility, we get the maximand as:

$$\text{Max EU } \{a, [p_a (Q - a) - wL^h + wF_2 + I]/p_m, T - F_1 - F_2\} \qquad (2.8)$$

Differentiating the maximand with respect to each of the arguments a, F_1, F_2 and L^h in turn,[7] we may write the optimizing conditions as:

$$E\{U_a - U_m p_a / p_m\} = 0 \qquad (2.9a)$$

$$E\{U_m g_L \epsilon p_a / p_m - U_l\} = 0 \qquad (2.9b)$$

$$E\{U_m w / p_m - U_l\} = 0 \qquad (2.9c)$$

$$E\{U_m g_L \epsilon p_a / p_m - w\} = 0 \qquad (2.9d)$$

which, using the rule $E(x, y) = E(x) E(y) + Cov(x, y)$ for random variables x and y, may be re-written as (Horowitz, 1970):

$$E(U_a) / E(U_m) = p_a / p_m \qquad (2.10a)$$

$$\bar{\epsilon} g_L p_a / p_m - E(U_l) / E(U_m) = -[Cov(U_m, \epsilon g_L)/E(U_m)](p_a / p_m) \quad (2.10b)$$

$$E(U_l) / E(U_m) = w / p_m \qquad (2.10c)$$

$$\bar{\epsilon} g_L p_a - w = -[Cov(U_m, \epsilon g_L)/E(U_m)]p_m \qquad (2.10d)$$

Equation (2.10a) tells us that the agricultural staple is consumed up to the point where the expected marginal rate of substitution between the consumption staple and the market purchased good equals their relative price ratio.[8] Equation (2.10b) tells us that the difference between the expected marginal rate of substitution between leisure and the market purchased good, and the expected value of the marginal product of labour is proportional to the risk premium associated with the covariance of U_m and ϵg_L. Equation (2.10c) says that off-farm labour supply is determined by the condition that the expected marginal rate of substitution be equal to the real wage. Note that on-farm labour supply, off-farm labour supply and leisure are tied together via the time constraint facing the household, so that risk considerations will also affect the determination of off-farm labour supply. Finally, (2.10d) says that the difference between the expected value of the marginal product of labour and the wage rate is proportional to the risk premium associated with the covariance of U_m and ϵg_L. Thus, both the off-farm supply of labour as well as the demand for labour are affected by the presence of production risk. What precisely is the effect that the latter has on the former is something that we shall now explore.

Critical Elements of the Model

From the above framework it is evident that the influence of production risk on farm household decision-making turns, presumably, on the interplay of two factors — first, the household's risk attitudes; and second, the risk regime, i.e. the manner in which risk enters the production function. The ensuing analysis considers each of these factors in turn.

Evidence on Risk Attitudes

Given that risk is an inherent part of most real world situations, its influence on the farm household's (firm's) decision-making turns on the decision agents' risk attitudes. If the agents were risk-neutral, then of course the presence of risk would be no cause for concern. Risk neutrality of farmers, however, does not seem to be a convincing conjecture for most situations involving 'nontrivial' payoffs. The presence of risk preference or risk aversion amongst agents, on the other hand, may have important implications for their behaviour, as is evident from the vast literature relating to decision-making under uncertainty. Why are some farmers much more willing to adopt new technologies than others (Feder, Just and Zilberman, 1985)? Why do some farmers fail to employ inputs up to the point of equality between its marginal product and real factor cost (Moscardi and de Janvry, 1977; Bardhan, 1973)? Why do some farmers assume large debts, while others (in the words of Halter and Beringer, 1960) appear to feel that 'a mortgage casts a shadow on the sunniest field'?

Further, insofar as attitudes to risk affect farm decision-making, not taking cognizance of risk-taking behaviour may have economy-wide implications (Hazell, 1982). Thus, if in fact farmers were risk averse, failure to account for this fact could result in, first, serious overestimation of the supply response of agricultural products. This follows from the fact that under risk aversion farmers would employ sub-optimal amounts of inputs and therefore produce sub-optimal amounts of output (Sandmo, 1971; Batra and Ullah, 1974). So that failure to allow for risk aversion would lead to an overestimation of the quantity of inputs used, and hence to an overestimation of the quantity of output produced. Second, as a corollary, this would naturally lead to upwards biased estimates of the supply elasticities of crops. Third, it would result in upwards biased estimates of the productivity of various inputs such as land, fertilizer, water etc. Fourth, it may lead to the advocacy of undesirably specialized cropping patterns. One of the ways in which risk averse farmers may attempt to cope with production risk is by opting for diverse cropping patterns. To the extent that the factor(s) making for production risk for a particular crop are not necessarily the same as those for another, a diversified cropping pattern would tend to limit the covariance of the production risks, and the farmers' overall incomes would be stabilised. By implication, if farmers are not risk averse, they would choose less diversified cropping patterns. Failure to allow for the farmers' risk aversion, therefore, would lead to the prescription of relatively specialized cropping patterns. Fifth, it may result in the advocacy of incorrect technology or input combinations. For instance, of two types of high yielding varieties available, one may offer relatively higher expected returns but may also exhibit a higher variance of returns. Given the choice, risk averse farmers may prefer to opt for the variety that gives them a more stable income. But if their risk attitudes are not allowed for, the prescription (from extension workers, say) may be for the adoption of the technology promising higher expected returns. To address such issues with sufficient cogency, therefore, one must grapple, *inter alia*, with issues of agents' risk preferences.

What then is a plausible, reasonably representative assumption about farmers' risk attitudes? Are they risk averse, risk neutral, or risk preferring? The rest of this section appraises the available empirical evidence to enable us to decide what could be a tenable assumption about farmers' risk attitudes. Some general observations are offered at the end of this section. Further, are these risk attitudes uniform across a given population or do they vary with the personal characteristics of the farmers in question? This important question is analysed in the appendix, since it is not important for the development of the estimable labour supply models. We have taken recourse to evaluating the extant evidence on risk attitudes, rather than measure them afresh, simply because this study cannot possibly test for all the hypotheses itself. At the same time, since non-risk neutrality is a crucial maintained hypothesis in our study of labour supply, we would not like to merely presume it by referring to 'the received literature' with a wave of the hand. As a mid-way strategy, we prefer to analyse the available evidence in some depth before making a judgement.

The past couple of decades have seen numerous attempts at eliciting farmers' risk preferences. We may categorize these various attempts as follows: (i) the interview method, (ii) the interview method with hypothetical payoffs, (iii) the interview method with actual payoffs, and (iv) the indirect method using observed data. We now consider the evidence which constitutes each of these categories.

(i) The Interview method One of the earliest studies attempting to gauge farmers' risk attitudes was that of Johnson (1962). He examined six studies that had been originally conducted to test the hypothesis that '... given an uncertain price farmers would discount the uncertainty by showing a willingness to contract forward at less than their expected price'. In each of these studies, samples of farmers were interviewed to elicit their price expectations for various commodities, as well as the minimum certain current price that they would be willing to accept in lieu of the uncertain expected price. An analysis of their responses showed that in five of these six studies, a majority of the farmers quoted a certain current price *as great as or greater than* the future expected, uncertain price (Table 2.1). While the responses from the remaining sixth study (not reported in Table 2.1) differed, this evidence was discounted on grounds of noncomparability with that of the other five studies.[9] In trying to rationalize the evidence, Johnson proffered the explanation that these farmers could be (or could be treated as) expected utility maximisers, in which case their responses would be compatible with risk preference.

In assessing the tenability of his own inference, Johnson claimed that '... neither bias nor communication problems vitiate the results ...'. Davidson and Mighell (1963) think otherwise. They argue that it was probably lack of experience with the kind of hypothetical contracting situations that the farmers were confronted with that determined their responses. Referring to other studies of farmers' response to risk in the '... same general geographic area', they report definite risk aversion on the part of the respondents. They conclude rather evocatively that: 'Thus, the 'six studies' tell us something valuable about farmers' reaction in an environment largely without contracts. Six more studies *in contracting areas* would probably tell us something different about reactions in an area accustomed to contracting' (italics ours).

Morrison and Judge (1955), one of the six studies reviewed by Johnson, offered a rather interesting reason why poultry farmers did not discount expected prices; an explanation curiously ignored by Johnson. They felt that the premium certain prices that the poultry farmers asked for was merely a strategy where the farmers would initially demand a higher price than they actually expected to get. Such behaviour is not uncommon

Table 2.1 Percentage distributions of risk attitudes: elicitation method (i)

Study	Region	Output	Sample Size	Averse (%)	Neutral (%)	Preferring (%)[a]
Brownlee-	USA	Corn,	49	2	12	51
Gainer		Soybeans	43	7	9	44
Williams	USA	Corn[b],	100	6	5	78
		Corn[c]	39	0	0	87
Boan	USA	Pigs,	10	4	0[d]	6
		Dairy				
Morrison-	USA	Eggs,	32	22	34	44
Judge		Broilers	15	13	13	73
Bramlett-	USA	Pigs	44	4	27	55
Johnson[e]						

[a] Percentages do not sum to 100 since some farmers would not answer the questions.
[b] Farmers 'in allotment', i.e. eligible to store corn under the government loan programme.
[c] Farmers not 'in allotment'.
[d] Results were reported for those willing to accept a certain price equal to or greater than the expected price.
[e] Bramlett and Johnson results taken from Johnson (1962, Table 2, p. 202).

between bargainers. For instance, the seller initially quotes a price higher than he actually expects to receive (and the purchaser initially quotes a price lower than he actually expects to pay). Therefore, the farmers' responses cannot be taken at face value to be responses to risk.

Insofar as agents derive utility from income and not from prices *per se*, the empirical evidence adduced by Johnson is meaningful only if there is a monotonic relationship between the prices received by farmers and their incomes. And in fact, Johnson does assume prices and incomes to have a one-to-one correspondence so that '... entrepreneurs can be considered as making decisions about income as a chance variable'. This assumption, however, may not be justified. To appreciate this consider, for instance, the circumstances under which farmers may be holding expectations that the price they are going to receive will be low. From the demand side, this expectation may have been the result of the prior expectation that demand will be low (given the output). Therefore, since both price and demand are expected to be depressed, we may expect the farmers' incomes to be depressed too. Alternatively, from the supply side, the expectation of a low price may be the result of the prior expectation that the harvest is going to be very good (given the demand). In this case, since price and output are moving in opposite directions it is not immediately clear whether income is going to be higher or lower. Consequently, price and income may not be monotonically related, so that one may not be justified in assuming from the empirical evidence presented by Johnson, that farmers are risk preferring. Perhaps taking their cue from Johnson's suggested explanation, a host of subsequent studies actually tried mapping out their respondents' preference functions. We consider these below.

(ii) The Interview method with hypothetical payoffs This approach essentially consists of interviewing individuals so as to elicit their most preferred choices from amongst a set of options involving hypothetical gains and losses. The basic or 'von Neumann-Morgenstern' model employed under this approach (Fishburn, 1967), involves the determination of points of indifference between risky options and their certainty equivalents. Given a series of such points, the whole utility function (i.e. utility as a function of money outcomes) may then be mapped out by regression analysis (Officer and Halter, 1968), free-hand drawing (Francisco and Anderson, 1972) or by some other approximation method. The shape of the curve so derived yields the necessary information on risk preferences. Thus, given a positive marginal utility of wealth, i.e. $U' > 0$, an agent is said to be risk averse, risk neutral or risk preferring according as: (a) U'' is less than, equal to or greater than zero.[10] Young (1979) points out that equivalent measures for risk preference classification are: (b) $\delta EU/\delta \sigma^2$, (c) $-U''/U'$, (d) $(d\mu/d\sigma^2)_{EU\ constant}$, and (e) the risk premium, i.e. the difference between the expected value of a risky prospect and its certainty equivalent. With measure (b) the risk preference classification is derived in the same way as with (a) above, but for (c), (d) and (e) the inequalities are reversed. From measure (c) or absolute risk aversion, Pratt (1964) also defined: (f) $-yU''/U'$ or relative risk aversion, where y is wealth. Another related measure is partial relative risk aversion which is defined as: (g) $-\Delta y.U''/U'$, where Δy is the change in wealth (Zeckhauser and Keeler, 1970; Menezes and Hanson, 1970). Downside risk aversion or aversion to the risk of falling below some critical level of wealth, is captured in a utility-theoretic

measure as: (h) U'''/U', for utility functions where $U'' > 0$ (Menezes, Geiss and Tressler, 1980).

Two variants of the above method have also been employed in the literature (Fishburn, 1967). The 'modified von Neumann-Morgenstern' method confronts the respondents with gains and losses having equal probabilities of one-half, while the 'Ramsey method' confronts the respondents with choices between risky outcomes only (rather than with choices between risky outcomes on the one hand and sure outcomes on the other). More on these variants later. While most of the empirical studies falling in this category use these expected utility techniques, the occasional study uses some non-expected utility technique. One such is the 'expected income-focus loss' method (Webster and Kennedy, 1975). The interview procedure is used to derive indifference curves involving trade-offs between expected income and focus loss income, where the latter is defined as the minimum income obtainable with some (small) pre-specified probability. The shape of the indifference curves then reveals the respondents' risk preferences. Another alternative employed is the so-called 'interval approach' (King and Robison, 1981; Wilson and Eidman, 1983). This is based on the principle of stochastic dominance which, unlike the single-argument utility function, does not restrict the preferred set to a single choice. This would be especially pertinent in situations where the difference between alternatives is small and could easily be due to measurement errors. Therefore, instead of deriving point estimates of risk aversion, they derive interval estimates of risk aversion. This is done as follows. On the assumption that the farmer possesses a constant absolute risk aversion utility function with respect to the decision variable (say, farm profits), pairs of distributions of farm profits are ordered for given upper and lower limits of the risk parameter. Given these orderings, the interview procedure is used to construct an interval measure of the farmer's risk parameter for a given level of farm profits. By varying the level of farm profits, the risk aversion function is then obtained.

One or more of these approaches have been employed by different authors in a range of diverse situations (Table 2.2, panel A). McCarthy and Anderson (1966) estimate utility functions for seventeen beef cattle farmers in Australia. Officer and Halter (1968) estimate various utility functions for a random sample of five wool producers in New South Wales, Australia. The decision problem was cast in terms of the amount of fodder stock that should be carried by the farmers, a monetarily small but most pressing problem in that drought-prone area. Francisco and Anderson (1972) used as subjects twenty-one pastoralists (wool producers) also in New South

Wales, Australia. While the sample selection was non-random, the hypothetical gambles they were given were representative of the scale of decisions taken by pastoralists in that area. Lin, Dean and Moore (1974) study six large California farms, which practised irrigated fruit, nut and vegetable cultivation. None of the farms was subject to a capital constraint as they had ample access to capital. Webster and Kennedy (1975) estimated utility functions for a sample of five sheep and grain producing farmers from New South Wales in Australia. Not much more sample information is provided in their study. Conklin, Baquet and Halter (1977) consider a group of eight orchardists in the state of Oregon, USA. Halter and Mason (1978) interviewed a larger group of 44 grass seed cultivators, also in Oregon, USA. Bond and Wonder (1980) apply this approach to a sample of 201 Australian farmers distributed over all the three agroclimatic zones (Pastoral, Wheat-sheep and High rainfall). Finally, Wilson and Eidman (1983) apply the interval approach to a purposively selected sample of 45 American farmers engaged in raising pigs. The purpose behind our brief description of these studies was to emphasize the wide range of farming situations covered, the size and nature of the samples used, and their wide geographic sweep.

All the studies considered above pertain to farmers in *developed* agriculture. Therefore, it may appear as if their results are not directly relevant to developing agriculture where production conditions are likely to be vastly more risky. On the contrary, however, these results may still be instructive. For if developed country farmers are found to be risk averse or even risk neutral, then it stands to reason that developing country farmers may be expected to be risk averse, considering that a large proportion of underdeveloped agriculture is characterised by rainfall dependent semi-arid/arid farming, and given the absence of well-developed credit, insurance and futures markets.

Even so, direct evidence about primary producers' risk aversion in *developing* countries would serve to make the issue clearer. Dillon and Scandizzo (1978) conducted their study in a semi-arid tropical region of Brazil (Table 2.2, panel B). Using a random sample of 130 share-owners and sharecroppers involved in crop production, two subsets of responses were collected for each group of peasants. In the first subset, while total income was risky, the minimum subsistence needs were covered. In the second subset, even the subsistence needs were at risk. Both subsets of experiments specified the probability of the 'good outcome' as 3/4 and that of the 'bad outcome' as 1/4. This sample of farmers was being surveyed for the third year in succession as part of a larger project, and the results of the

Table 2.2 Percentage distributions of risk attitudes: elicitation method (ii)

Panel A

Study	Region	Output	Sample Size	Averse (%)	Neutral (%)	Preferring (%)[a]
McCarthy-Anderson	Australia	Cattle	17 VNM[b]	48	29	23
Officer-Halter	Australia	Wool	5 MVNM1[c]	60	20	20
			5 RAM1[d]	20	0	60
			5 MVNM2[c]	40	40	0
			5 RAM2[d]	80	0	20
Francisco-Anderson	Australia	Wool	21 VNM	0	0	5
Lin-Dean-Moore	USA	Fruits, nuts, vegetables	6 VNM	50	33	0
Webster-Kennedy	Australia	Sheep, grain	5 MVNM	100	0	0
			5 EF[e]	80	0	0
Conklin-Baquet-Halter	USA	Fruit	8 VNM	37	0	13
Halter-Mason	USA	Grass seed	44 VNM	33	33	33
Bond-Wonder	Australia	Crops, Animals	217 VNM	35	15	12
Wilson-Eidman	USA	Swine	45 IA[f]	44	34	22

Panel B

Dillon-Scandizzo	Brazil	Crops	56 O-SA[g]	70	9	21
			47 S-SA[h]	58	8	34
			56 O-SR[g]	87	0	13
			47 S-SR[h]	79	0	21

[a] Some percentages do not sum to 100 because of mixed (i.e. risk averse and risk preferring responses.
[b] VNM denotes the von Neumann-Morgenstern model.

Table 2.2   continued

[c] MVNM1, MVNM2 denote the modified VNM model in years 1 and 2, respectively.
[d] RAM1, RAM2 denote the Ramsey model in years 1 and 2, respectively.
[e] EF denotes the 'expected income-focus loss' model.
[f] IA denotes the 'interval approach'.
[g] O-SA, O-SR denote 'Owners-Subsistence Assured' and 'Owners-Subsistence at risk'.
[h] S-SA, S-SR denote 'Sharecroppers-Subsistence Assured' and 'Sharecroppers-Subsistence at risk'.

third year's responses were used in the estimation of risk attitudes. They were interviewed by the same set of researchers in all three years. These researchers were agricultural economics graduates and were local to that area. Thus, care was taken to ensure that the farmers were familiar with the surveyors and survey methods, and that a good rapport existed between the surveyors and respondents.

In spite of the fact that the various authors (in developed as well as developing country studies) often took a lot of trouble in conducting the interviews with the farmers, this approach could (and often turned out to) be a potential prey to several shortcomings:

(a) It could be subject to interviewer bias. In fact, this was found to be true in an experiment carried out by Binswanger (1980) in the Indian context. Using a large sample of cultivators in the Indian semi-arid tropics (more on his sample below), he found that the farmers in village Shirapur turned out to be significantly more risk averse then those in the neighbouring village of Kalman when these villages were interviewed by investigators B and A, respectively, However, when these villages were resurveyed a month later, switching investigators and their time sequences of investigation, the farmers in village Kalman were now found to be more risk averse than those in village Shirapur. It seemed that investigator B tended to classify respondents as more risk averse than investigator A. A resurvey of all the six villages in the sample resulted in a radical reclassification of individuals between positive and negative risk aversion in more than 20% of the cases. Thus, interview-based techniques are inevitably dogged by the problem of investigator pre-disposition. Of course, the problem really arises because different investigators possess different degrees of pre-disposition.

(b) Individuals may not have sufficient incentive to reveal their *true* preferences. This follows from the fact that hypothetical situations, by definition, do not involve actual gains and losses for the interviewees. On the one hand, therefore, they stand to receive no monetary gain from participating in what must often be rather tedious 'games'. And on the other, since they do not actually make any monetary losses, in all probability they do not really feel the pinch of losing the games. Therefore, despite sincere efforts at imagining oneself in a given hypothetical situation, the very nature of that hypothetical situation may prevent the interviewees from revealing their *true* preferences.

(c) Even if they have incentive enough to reveal their true preferences, they may be *unable* to do so vis-à-vis situations they have neither experienced nor contemplated. To take this problem one step backwards, the early psychology literature was guilty of basing risk attitude elicitation on 'test-tube experiments' involving situations which had little relevance to real-life situations (Tversky, 1967). Presumably, this would render the visualisation of such situations by the interviewees even more difficult. But even in the context of real-life situations, a subject would be in a position to properly evaluate an option only if he has had some prior experience of it in the first place, and sufficient time to think about it. This is precisely the point of criticism that Davidson and Mighell (1963) raised about the studies examined by Johnson (1962) above — namely, that the farmers being questioned about forward contracts had not, for the most part, been exposed to such contracting situations. Further, before taking any significant decisions, individuals usually think about them and may also discuss them with friends, relatives or even professionals (say, extension workers in the case of farmers). This opportunity of prolonged evaluation is not usually available to respondents participating in mind experiments. Consequently, they may be unable to properly evaluate the situations posed to them and hence unable to reveal their true preferences.

(d) The concept of probability is hardly intuitively obvious, even when presented in frequency terms. While a college student may be able to use the stated probabilities in working out the relevant mathematical expectations, the 'lay-person' may, at best, merely use them as indicators of the 'relative likelihood' of the different outcomes. This criticism is probably more applicable to less developed economies where the levels of education generally, and those of farmers particularly, are very low.

(e) The individuals' responses may be affected by the manner in which the questions are posed. For instance, if a farmer is told that in a given situation he would be able to *harvest 90% of his crop*, his response might be different from what it might be if he is alternatively told that he would *lose 10% of his crop*.

(f) The individuals may exhibit probability preferences. The psychology literature provides ample evidence that individuals' subjective probabilities may diverge from the objective probabilities of the outcomes they face. so that we may find that individuals attach different subjective probabilities to the same objective probability (Tversky, 1967).

Some of the studies try to circumvent this problem by using 'neutral probabilities', i.e. a probability of one-half for both gains and losses. This is called the 'modified von Neumann-Morgenstern approach' as noted above. While this may remove the bias on account of probability preferences, by definition it does not cover decision-making behaviour under situations where the probabilities of gain and loss are not the same. And arguably, the latter situations probably predominate in actuality.

(g) The individuals may well derive different degrees of utility or disutility from gambling *per se*, the very method utilised for eliciting preferences. Since the individuals are asked to choose between a sure outcome and a gamble, if they hold a positive or negative bias towards gambling they may be predisposed against or in favour of the sure alternative. Some researchers attempt to get around this hurdle by confronting their subjects with choices involving risky alternatives only. This is termed the 'Ramsey model' (which, in addition, uses equal probabilities for gains and losses). But while this does away with the bias against gambling in a situation where the subject is confronted with a choice between a sure outcome and a risky alternative, it does not necessarily do away with the bias against gambling *per se*. Thus, a player who dislikes gambling may not be properly motivated to participate in such a study to begin with.

(h) The choice of utility function may turn out to be significant. This problem has two aspects. Usually it is assumed that the utility function is quadratic, or that its argument (say, money income) is a normally distributed random variable rendering the utility function quadratic anyway, or else that the utility function is expressed as a function of the first two moments of 'money income' only as a (first-order Taylor series) approximation. But even when only the first two moments are taken to be relevant, Lin and Chang (1978) show that the choice of *functional form* (that is, whether it is linear in these moments, or log-linear etc.) can have important implications.

(i) The assumption that utility can be reduced to a function of a single argument in terms of money income may be unjustifiable. There might well be other important considerations that determine an individual's utility, and ignoring these while estimating the risk preference parameters may lead to considerable bias.

(j) The sample size will perforce have to be small, since each respondent needs to be questioned individually and with sufficient rigour. This will be especially true where the subjects need to be kept track of over time. This will limit, however, the general applicability of the results obtained. Where the sample sizes are especially small, the sampling error is likely to be especially large, diminishing our confidence in the results obtained.

(k) Finally, it is argued by some that expected utility theory is inadmissible as a descriptive theory of economic behaviour because there are many situations where preferences violate the axioms underlying the expected utility paradigm (Kahneman and Tversky, 1979). Note, first of all, that this is not a criticism of interview-based techniques *per se*. Moreover, the demonstration of the above-mentioned violations is itself based on responses to *hypothetical* choice problems. In any case, there is a large literature discussing this issue, and we do not intend to discuss it here (Schoemaker, 1982; Machina, 1989).

(iii) The Interview method with actual payoffs In an attempt to overcome some of the shortcomings of the interview-based method discussed above, Binswanger (1978, 1980) conducted a series of *in vivo* experiments involving actual payoffs to the respondents (Table 2.3). An important aspect of his experiments was that the payoffs were '... large enough to induce participants to reveal their preferences'. For instance, the highest payoff exceeded the monthly income of an unskilled agricultural labourer. His study covered 330 individuals selected at random from six villages in (rural) Maharashtra and Andhra Pradesh states in India. The individuals were offered eight alternative choices involving a trade-off between expected return and its standard deviation. Each alternative consisted of a 'good' and 'bad' outcome, with associated probabilities of one-half. To counter moral problems associated with gambling, the returns promised for the various alternatives were such that the worst possible outcome would be a zero gain. The various alternatives were arbitrarily labelled to indicate the associated degree of risk aversion, where risk aversion was defined both in terms of the coefficient of variation of returns as well as the coefficient of partial risk aversion. To allow for the possibility that risk attitudes may depend on the stakes involved, experiments involving 'low' and 'high' stakes

Table 2.3 Percentage distributions of risk attitudes: elicitation method (iii)

Study	Region	Output	Sample Size	Averse (%)	Neutral (%)	Preferring (%)[a]
Binswanger	India	Crops	119(Rs.0.5)[b]	71	0	19
			117 (Rs. 5)	84	0	9
			118 (Rs.50)	89	0	2
			118(Rs500)[c]	97	0	1
Walker	El Salvador	Maize	42 (C 0.5)	58	0	24
			42 (C 5.0)	77	0	8
			42 (C 10)	77	0	10
Binswanger -	Phillipines	Rice	49 (P 50)[d]	84	0	16
Sillers			49 (P 500)[d]	86	0	14
			49 (P 50)[d]	90	0	10
Grisley-	Thailand	Rice	39 (B 66.6)	92	0	8
Kellogg			39 (B 200)	100	0	0

[a] Percentages do not sum to 100 in the Binswanger and Walker studies because some responses were categorised as 'inefficient'. Binswanger-Sillers disregarded the inefficient responses.
[b] Rs., C, P and B denote the currencies Rupees, Colon, Peso and Baht, respectively.
[c] The Rs. 500 experiment used hypothetical payoffs. These results have been included here for completeness.
[d] These games had outcomes allowing for gains only.
[e] These games had outcomes allowing for both gains and losses.

were carried out. These were called the 'Rs. 0.5 game', 'Rs. 5 game', 'Rs. 50 game' and 'Rs. 500 game'. The experiments were conducted seven or eight times, over a period of six weeks or more. They were spread out over time, so as to facilitate familiarisation, reflection and discussion. Walker (1981) replicated Binswanger's technique to look at the risk preferences of 42 maize farmers in two villages of northern El Salvador. Binswanger and Sillers (1983) tried to improve upon Binswanger's method by considering experiments that allowed for losses as well. They also allowed for unequal probabilities of outcomes in their experiments.[11] Grisley and Kellogg (1987) allowed for a larger number of alternatives in their application of

Binswanger's method than did Binswanger, to obtain relatively precise estimates of the risk preferences of 39 rice farmers in the Chiang Mai valley of northern Thailand.

While this approach seems to overcome some of the shortcomings of the interview method that we noted above, it is still susceptible to at least some of the others. Moreover, not all experiments can involve significant payments to respondents (Robison, 1982).[12] Thus, for instance, the 'Rs. 500 experiments' in Binswanger's study and the 'Colon 50 experiments' in Walker's study involved hypothetical payoffs. Further, these studies generally do not consider experiments which allow for losses, thereby precluding outright risk preferring behaviour by construction. An exception is Binswanger and Siller's study where, however, the potential losses in the 'gains and losses' experiments were covered by giving a sum of money to the players several days before the game. But playing with other people's money may not reveal the risk attitudes that one might exhibit with one's own money.

(iv) The Indirect method using observed data The advantage of the indirect or econometric approach to eliciting risk attitudes stems from the fact that it makes use of the data emanating from the actual decisions made by producers. Risk attitudes are gauged by comparing the actual input demands or output supply under risky conditions with those that would result under conditions without risk. The use of actual data is claimed to automatically take care of many of the criticisms levelled against the interview-based approaches. By definition it would not be subject to interviewer bias simply because no *interviews per se* are involved. The surveyors enter the picture merely as data collectors. Again, by definition, 'framing effects', lack of familiarity with the concepts of probability and expectation, probability preferences, and moral attitudes to gambling would not be contentious issues. Further, since the actual decisions being analysed are related to the livelihoods of the sample agents, and are hence not trivial, one would not expect problems of insufficient incentives, lack of experience with the situations at hand, or insufficient time and opportunity for reflection and discussion, to vitiate the results of this approach. Finally, since secondary data will mostly suffice for this approach, sample sizes can be large both in the cross-section as well as the time series dimensions. And if at all this approach is sought to be used in the context of the expected utility paradigm, the utility function need not be a single argument function of money income alone (see below). In other words, in many respects this approach is likely to be an improvement over the interview-

Table 2.4   Percentage distributions of risk attitudes: elicitation method (iv)

Study	Region	Output	Sample Size	Averse (%)	Neutral (%)	Preferring (%)
Moscardi-deJanvry	Mexico	Corn	45	100	0	0
Brink-McCarl	USA	Corn	38	66	34	0
Shahabuddin et.al.	Bangladesh	Crops	202 (R)[a]	65	0	35
			202 (C)[a]	77	0	23
Antle (1987)	India	Rice	282	100	0	0
Bardsley-Harris	Australia	Crops, Animals	413	100	0	0
Antle (1989)	India	Crops	350	61	39[b]	0

[a] R denotes 'reported data', and C 'computed data'.
[b] The proportion of the sample falling in this category is conjectural (see Antle, 1989).

based ones discussed above.

One of the earliest empirical studies using the econometric approach was conducted by Moscardi and de Janvry (1977) (Table 2.4). Defining risk in terms of a safety first principle (that production decisions are undertaken such that subsistence needs are covered), they estimated a risk aversion parameter by comparing the optimum and actual fertilisation levels of 45 sampled farmers in Puebla, Mexico. Brink and McCarl (1978) constructed a linear programming portfolio choice model for 38 large farmers in the United States cornbelt, wherein risk is defined as negative deviation from the expected return. Their risk preferences were then measured in terms of the difference between their actual acreages under production and those suggested by the programming model. Significance tests were conducted to test the null hypothesis that risk aversion makes no difference to the acreage allocations. Shahabuddin *et.al.* (1986) constructed a safety-first model to estimate the risk attitudes of a large sample of 202 multi-crop farmers in four districts of Bangladesh. Antle (1987) estimated the parameters of the distribution of risk attitudes for a large sample of 282 observations over the period 1975-76/1980-81 pertaining to a sample of 30 farmers growing irrigated rice in a village in south-central India. He used a moment-based approximation to the joint distribution of profits and risk pertinent to these farmers, within an expected utility framework. The labour input equation was used to estimate the moments of the producers' risk attitudes since it was felt that labour use (unlike the use of other inputs such as fertilizer) was not constrained by access to credit. Risk attitudes themselves were measured in terms of the coefficient of absolute risk aversion, downside risk aversion and the risk premium. Bardsley and Harris (1987) constructed a simple model that unifies the production and consumption decisions of farmers via their financing decisions. This results in a small system of simultaneous equations, which is solved on the assumption that farmers choose the optimal mean-variance combination on the efficiency frontier. Using 413 observations spanning the period 1977-78/1981-82, they estimated the coefficient of partial risk aversion for a group of Australian pastoralists. Antle (1989) observed that his earlier approach (Antle, 1987), as indeed all 'structural' approaches, made very heavy demands on the data required. To remedy this, he proposed a 'nonstructural' approach. Under the assumption that producers make optimal production decisions, he argued that their attitudes towards risk result in (consistent) changes in the moments of the distribution of net returns. By estimating these changes over time, the producers' underlying risk attitudes may be discerned. He employed this procedure with 350 observations pertaining to 70 farmers over the period 1976-77/1981-82, in three villages in the Indian semi-arid tropics. Risk attitudes were approximated by the coefficients of absolute and downside risk aversion.

Although this approach (i.e. the indirect method using observed data) is relatively superior to the interview-based approaches on a number of counts, as we noted above, it is subject to a serious criticism. Since it seeks to measure risk preferences in terms of the difference between actual and optimal decisions, it ascribes to risk attitudes this entire difference. Instead, however, a number of other causes such as imperfect capital markets, imperfect information, restricted access to inputs etc. could be at the root of such differences (Moscardi and de Janvry, 1977). It is not very clear, therefore, which of the measurement techniques discussed above is the 'most preferred'. In other words, it may not be possible to first choose the most preferable method of measurement of risk attitudes from amongst those available, and *then* repose one's faith in the results emanating from the use of that method to the exclusion of the other methods. Given the nascent state of research in this area, it might be more advisable to consider the implications of all the results at our disposal (excepting, of course, those that we have argued should not be considered for one reason or another).

Some Generalisations

From a perusal of the results it appears that a 'fair' proportion of the farmers in developed countries are relatively risk preferring. More correctly, it seems that compared to the developing countries a larger percentage of farmers in the developed countries are risk preferring. This figure probably falls in the range of 20% to 33%,[13] which does not bear out Young's (1979, p. 1067) observation that '[A]mong the studies of Australian and American farmers, approximately 50% of the sampled individuals manifested risk preferring attitudes ...'. Unfortunately, the studies surveyed used very small samples of farmers. Thus, eight of the nine studies in Table 2.2, panel A report a sample size of between five and 45 only. Worse still, often these samples were of a non-random nature. Consequently, the sampling errors in these studies may be large and their results need to be further confirmed before we can repose confidence in them.

Second, the farmers in developing agriculture appear to be predominantly risk averse. While this observation follows automatically from the first observation, it needs to be highlighted and discussed separately. Most of the studies pertinent to this observation (Table 2.2, panel B; Table 2.3 and Table 2.4) were carried out with substantially large samples. Furthermore, these samples were randomly chosen for the most part, and a lot of pains seem to have been taken to ensure that data were collected from the respondents only after prolonged familiarisation with the interviewers and their techniques. One is inclined to place, therefore, a fair amount of confidence in these studies.

Third, as the payoff levels rise above 'trivial' amounts, farmers (in developing countries) become more and more risk averse (Table 2.3). Binswanger (1980, p. 406) goes further and concludes that at relatively high payoff levels '... risk aversion is highly concentrated at the intermediate and moderate levels ...', a 'finding' that is echoed by others (see Walker, 1981). However, we feel that this conclusion is somewhat by assumption, since the various risk aversion classes that these researchers define (such as 'slight', 'moderate', 'intermediate' etc.) are arbitrary. This objection is important because their conclusion leads to the erroneous claim (which may well be supported by *other* evidence, however), that farmers are mostly 'moderately' risk averse and not 'extremely' risk averse (Walker,

1981, p. 85). If we were to apportion the risk averse farmers into only two categories — 'low risk aversion' comprising the 'slight' and 'moderate' classes, and 'high risk aversion' comprising the 'intermediate', 'severe' and 'extreme' classes, a categorisation not any more arbitrary than the original — we would find that even at relatively high payoff levels the proportion of farmers in the 'high risk aversion' category is not much smaller than that in the 'low risk aversion' category. Thus, in Binswanger's study, for the 'Rs. 50 level' game, 42.4% of the farmers would fall in the high-risk-aversion class whereas 46.6% would fall in the low-risk-aversion class. Indeed, for the 'Rs. 500 level' game, while only 28.8% of the farmers would fall in the low-risk-aversion class as many as 67.8% would fall in the high-risk-aversion class.[14]

The Risk Regime

We had noted above, that the influence of the presence of risk on household decision-making turns on the interplay between risk attitudes and the risk regime. We now turn to a discussion of the second factor, namely the manner in which risk is specified in the model. It seems to matter greatly whether risk enters the production function additively or multiplicatively. It is difficult to say, *a priori*, which of the two is the more plausible assumption. Newbery and Stiglitz (1981) interpret additive risk as implying that '[R]ain destroys a constant *amount* regardless of the size of the total crop ...' and multiplicative risk as implying that '[R]ain at harvest time leads to spoilage which is a constant *fraction* of the crop, regardless of its size ...' (emphasis added). But this is not instructive in telling us whether, for a given farmer, we should start off by assuming an additive risk structure or a multiplicative one. Suppose, for instance, that a given farmer's plot is struck by blight, as a result of which a certain amount of the crop is destroyed, irrespective of whether the total crop size is x or $100x$. Posed in this way, an additive risk structure would seem appropriate. However, we know that the farmer's total crop size is either x or $100x$. Suppose it is x. Then the *amount* of output destroyed by the blight may be expressed, alternatively, as a *fraction* of the total output. Thus, it becomes impossible to determine whether the true underlying structure was additive or multiplicative. While these arguments have been couched in terms of negative risks, they should also hold in the case of positive risks (which, for example, result in a bumper crop). Further, Newbery and Stiglitz point out that even if we assume additive risk at the micro-level, when we aggregate to obtain total output for all the farmers, we are in effect making total risk proportional to the total output. But this brings us back to a multiplicative specification. For this reason, they recommend the latter. The literature on household production models serves to focus on other important aspects of this problem. We look at some of these in the following analysis.

Labour Supply Functions and the Demand for Labour Function for Cultivator Households

Making, alternatively, the assumptions of additive and multiplicative revenue risk, we explore what effect these assumptions might have on the structure of the household production model and the specification of the off-farm labour supply functions and the demand for labour function derivable therefrom.

Proposition 1 In the presence of additive revenue risk, the farm household production model is separable, irrespective of whether the household is risk neutral or not. Of course, our interest lies in risk averse households.

Proof As Fabella (1989) shows, given additive revenue risk the first order conditions are the same as before, except that ϵ drops out.

$$E(U_a) / E(U_m) = p_a / p_m \tag{2.11a}$$

$$g_L \, p_a / p_m - E(U_l) / E(U_m) = -[Cov(U_m, g_L)/E(U_m)](p_a / p_m) \tag{2.11b}$$

$$E(U_l) / E(U_m) = w / p_m \tag{2.11c}$$

$$g_L \, p_a - w = -[Cov(U_m, g_L)/E(U_m)]p_m \tag{2.11d}$$

The term $Cov(U_m, \epsilon g_L)$, which is now equal to $Cov(U_m, g_L)$, degenerates to 0 since g_L is now deterministic. As a result, the last condition gives us $g_L \, p_a - w = 0$. But this is the usual static efficiency condition for the employment of factor L. Since this condition is independent of the consumption-side parameters (such as a, m etc.), the model is separable. (Q.E.D)

  Given additive risk, the household is unable to mitigate risk through variations in its factor use. This is reflected by the fact that the optimisation conditions do not contain any term in ϵ, the risk element. While this may seem to be an advantage for estimation purposes, as Fabella (*ibid.*) points out, it also destroys the homogeneity property of the production function, preventing the use of any duality techniques predicated on this property. These reasons, additionally, advocate the use of a multiplicative risk specification. Therefore, we consider it preferable to incorporate revenue risk in a multiplicative form.

Proposition 2 In the presence of multiplicative revenue risk, risk aversion (as indeed, non-risk neutrality in general) implies that the farm household production model is not separable.

Proof Using the optimisation conditions (2.10a)-(2.10d) derived earlier for multiplicative risk, and following Fabella (1989), note that when ϵ increases so does ϵg_L. This also increases (expected) profits and hence m, and so decreases U_m given risk aversion (i.e. $U_{mm} < 0$). Thus, $Cov(U_m, \epsilon g_L) < 0$, so that from equation (2.10d), $\epsilon g_L p_a - w \neq 0$. Moreover, EU_m is a function of the 'consumption side' variables. From (2.10d), therefore, the demand for labour (family plus hired) is a function of the consumption-side variables. In other words, this equation system is nonseparable and all the endogenous variables will have to be solved for simultaneously (Q.E.D)

A simultaneous equations estimation based on the assumption of nonseparability is attempted by Kanwar (1991), using household data collected by the International Crops Research Institute for the Semi-Arid Tropics (ICRISAT). The ICRISAT economists indicated, however, that the consumption data (which are required for the estimation of the nonseparable model) are relatively unreliable.[15] Hence, one would preferably like to eschew its use. Moreover, estimation of the nonseparable model is even otherwise fairly burdensome. Considering that the data and estimation requirements of a simultaneous equations system tend to be very heavy, various means have been adopted to characterise a simpler solution (Singh, Squire and Strauss, 1986, p. 22). Roe and Graham-Tomasi (1986) assume an additively separable utility function and independent production shocks over time (since they were considering a dynamic situation), to derive a separable model. On these assumptions one may characterise the problem as if the household sought to maximise its certainty equivalent income and then to choose the levels of consumption of goods and leisure. The production and consumption sides of the model may be taken to be separable in the sense that they are recursively determined — the production decisions of the household are undertaken first (specifically, the demand for labour), and the consumption decisions follow (specifically, the demand for leisure and hence the supply of labour). However, their assumptions may be perceived as too restrictive.

Alternatively, one may follow Fabella (*ibid.*) in pointing out that the multiplicative risk formulation used above is not satisfactory since it implies that an increase in any of the inputs increases risk (i.e. the variance of output), at the margin. For $Var(Q) = g_j^2 var(\epsilon)$ so that $\delta Var(Q)/\delta j = 2g_j var(\epsilon) > 0$ for all j. To allow for risk reducing inputs (such as irrigation), the production function may be specified as follows (Just and Pope, 1978; Pope and Kramer, 1979):

$$Q = g(x) + h(x)\epsilon \qquad g_j > 0, \ g_{jj} < 0, \ h_j < 0, \ E(\epsilon) = 0 \qquad (2.12)$$

Fabella shows, however, that this function may not be well-behaved and may even exhibit a *negative* marginal product for finite output. Only for 'higher and higher' input use with (a modified form of) such a production function do we have $g_L p_a - w \rightarrow 0$, i.e. the system is asymptotically separable. What input levels are 'high enough', however, is not quite clear.

In light of the above arguments, we prefer to adopt the following strategy. Having incorporated multiplicative risk in our model, we first test for the separability of production and consumption decisions. In other words, instead of *assuming* separability on one ground or another we *test* for it. Only subsequently do we proceed to estimate the relationships we are interested in. Note from first order condition *2.10d* above, that in the presence of risk the (expected) marginal product is not equated to the wage rate in determining the demand for labour. Here labour refers to family plus hired labour. Since $E(U_m)$ is a function of the consumption side variables, the demand for labour is a function of the consumption side variables as well. Since these consumption side variables, in turn, are contingent on the measures of household composition such as family size and the age and sex composition of the family, non-separation implies that the demand for labour by the household is a function of the demographic variables (Benjamin, 1992; Pollak and Wales, 1981). Therefore, to test for separation, we will simply test (see chapter 5 below) whether the demographic variables are significant determinants of the household demand for labour (holding constant the wage rate and the other exogenous variables). If indeed separation holds, then we would not need to solve system 2.10a-2.10d simultaneously for all the endogenous variables in the model. Tentatively capturing revenue risk by the coefficient of variation of net revenue (CVNR), the unconditional reduced-form demand for labour function may be written as:

$$L = L (w/p_m, p_a/p_m, I, Z_1, Z_2, CVNR)$$

or, alternatively, as:

$$L = L (RWR, ROP, I, Z_1, Z_2, CVNR) \qquad (2.13)$$

where *RWR* is the real wage rate w/p_m, and *ROP* is the real output price p_a/p_m (these variables being re-named merely for convenience).

Given separation, we may *then* estimate the unconditional off-farm labour supply function for cultivator households as:

$$F_2 = F_2 (RWR, ROP, I, Z_1, Z_2, CVNR)$$

This function specifies the *actual* supply of wage labour as a function of the *actual* real wage rate. Given the presence of involuntary unemployment in developing country rural labour markets, however, we feel that it would be more pertinent to consider the *desired* supply of labour, i.e. the actual off-farm labour supply plus the involuntary unemployment. Correspondingly, the wage variable should be taken to be the *expected* real wage rate, i.e. the product of the actual wage rate and the probability of finding employment in the casual labour market. The reduced form function for the *desired* supply of off-farm labour for cultivator households may be written as:

$$F_2^* = F_2^* (ERWR, ROP, I, Z_1, Z_2, CVNR) \qquad (2.14)$$

where F_2^* is the desired supply of off-farm labour by cultivator households, and *ERWR* is the expected real wage rate.

Labour Supply Function for Landless Households

While the primary focus of this study is the off-farm labour supply and labour demand behaviour of cultivator households, we now briefly consider the labour supply relation pertinent to landless households, this being the most important group of labour suppliers in the rural labour markets numerically. The analysis need only be brief because this case is much simpler than that of cultivator households. Unlike cultivator households which are both consumers and producers of their staples, landless or agricultural labour households are only consumers of their staples. Therefore, instead of the farm household model we can use the simpler representative consumer framework to consider the demand for leisure or the supply of labour on the part of the agricultural labour households. Difficult issues such as endogenous income determination (since income now accrues from the supply of wage labour only and not from self-cultivation as well), the separability between consumption and production decisions, and the effect of production risk on self-cultivation will not, therefore, enter the picture in this case. Production risk may, however, influence the availability of labour market opportunities. The availability of such opportunities to the landless households in a given village in a given year, may be proxied by the coefficient of variation of net revenue averaged over all the *cultivator* households in that village in that year.[16] Without repeating the formal derivation of the relation for landless households, and using the same symbols for convenience and ease of comparison (with the cultivator households' functions), we may specify their reduced form labour supply function as:

$$F_2 = F_2 \, (RWR, I, Z_1, AVCVNR)$$

which, in turn, may be expressed in terms of desired labour supply as:

$$F_2^* = F_2^* \, (ERWR, I, Z_1, AVCVNR) \tag{2.15}$$

where F_2^* is the desired supply of off-farm labour by landless households, *ERWR* is the expected real wage rate, and *AVCVNR* is the average coefficient of variation of net revenue.

Notes

1   'Small cultivators' were defined as households operating less than 2.5 acres, and having cultivation as their major occupation.
2   'Cultivators' were defined as households operating 0.1 acres or more, and having cultivation as their major occupation.
3   The comparison is somewhat vitiated by the fact that none of the other variables in these two equations were the same.
4   This follows from the fact that in a Cobb-Douglas production function, $\partial Q / \partial (farmdays) \, \partial (education) > 0$. Therefore, schooling shifts up the

demand for on-farm labour. Given the wage rate, this implies a *decline* in off-farm labour (unless schooling induces a decline in leisure by a large enough magnitude).

5   Bardhan (1984a) felt that given the ultra-conservative social norms in the Indian villages, where it is not considered particularly honourable that the household women be exposed to extra-mural labour, caste factors may be relatively important in explaining female labour supply response.

6   This formulation does not settle all the questions about the simultaneous hiring-in and hiring-out behaviour of developing country farmers (certainly in India). We feel that factors other than the wage rate are also operating to determine the hiring-in and hiring-out behaviour of farm households. For instance, time may become available for off-farm work in piecemeal fashion. To simplify, at sowing and harvest times there may be great demand for labour so that there is no time for off-farm work and labour may actually be hired in. But in-between sowing and harvesting the intensity of farm operations may be low enough to permit hiring out of family labour. In the aggregate, the farm household would be seen as both hiring-in and hiring-out labour, at wage w, simultaneously. Such complexities, however, are beyond the scope of the present work.

7   Land allocation is not treated endogenously because evidence shows that for our sample of households leasing in/leasing out was not really important. For details see chapter 5. Further, the respondents did not cite 'interlinked transactions' as a significant reason for whatever little leasing in/leasing out occurred (Jodha, 1984). This keeps the maximand simple.

8   The left hand side of (2.10a) is not exactly the expected marginal rate of substitution, but is actually the marginal rate of expected substitution. However, the discrepancy is likely to be small and may be overlooked.

9   Johnson felt that the results from this sixth study were confounded on account of support programmes benefitting the farmers. Income guarantees of this sort prevent a proper manifestation of market risk faced by the farmers.

10   As usual, a single prime (') denotes the first derivative with respect to the argument in question, a double prime denotes the second derivative etc.

11   In evaluating the results of Binswanger and Sillers' study presented in Table 2.3, note that they estimate the percentage distribution of

farmers' risk attitudes after excluding the 'inefficient' responses, i.e. choices which involved the same expected gain as the alternative but a higher variance of returns. We feel that this procedure is incorrect. If the inefficient responses were also to be included in the total responses, both the percentage of farmers preferring risk as well as those averse to risk would be smaller in magnitude.

12 On this issue, note the interesting view of Juster (1972), quoted in Bessler (1979): '[E]conomists are not accustomed to thinking in terms of these orders of magnitude (millions of dollars), but I suggest we take a page from the books of our brethren in the physical sciences. Particle accelerators and astronomical observatories that cost in the tens of millions are not uncommon, and they are judged to be worth their cost. Yet one is simply a way to generate observations, and the other is a way to measure observable physical phenomena'.

13 From Table 2.2 we notice that in one of the developed country samples the percentage of risk preferring farmers was as high as 60%, and in another as low as 5%. We treat these as outliers.

14 One other hypothesis may be pointed out for further study. Dillon and Scandizzo (1978) find that owners are more risk averse than sharecroppers. Since this is the only study shedding light on this issue, we are unable to attempt a generalisation.

15 Personal communication of the author with Dr. Tom Walker, (then) Principal Economist, ICRISAT.

16 For the production uncertainty that affects self-cultivation by the cultivator households also affects the labour market, irrespective of whether the labour market is supplied by labour from the cultivator households or the landless households.

Appendix: Risk Preferences and Socioeconomic Characteristics

We saw that despite the fact that an overwhelming proportion of farmers in developing agriculture are risk averse, there is still a fairly large proportion spanning the spectrum from risk neutrality to outright risk preference. Naturally, this leads one to ask whether this variation is systematically associated with differences in socioeconomic characteristics across individuals. Although the studies measuring risk aversion *per se* were seen to be fairly numerous, rather few of these went on to consider the above-mentioned association. In this appendix we briefly review the latter set to see if we can discern any systematic relationships from them. Since this is a digression, the reader may choose to proceed to the next chapter in order to maintain continuity.

Dillon and Scandizzo (1978) singled out five regressor variables '...for which data were available ...'. These were family net total income, farmer's age, household size, a dummy variable to reflect attitudes to betting (= 1 if gambling is considered immoral and 0 otherwise), and a risk variable. The dependent variable was risk premium. Separate regressions were estimated for owners and sharecroppers for both situations, i.e. 'subsistence at risk' as well as 'subsistence assured' (see the discussion above for details). The coefficient signs and significance levels are noted in Table 2.5. The results are fairly consistent although not always statistically significant. In the more realistic situation of subsistence at risk (columns 1, 2, 3, 4), a higher family income consistently implies lower risk aversion, whereas both a higher age and risk imply a higher risk aversion. Many of these relationships are significant. Again, a larger family size as well as an ethical dislike for gambling seem to result in higher risk aversion (although there is some contrary evidence in both cases).

Binswanger (1980) used a large number of regressors to explain risk aversion at each of the four 'game levels' (Table 2.6, panel A). For the lower level games, he reported more than one regression. The regressors were wealth (measured by gross sales value of physical assets), education,

Table 2.5 Risk preferences and socioeconomic characteristics[a]

Dependent variable: Risk premium

Regressor	Subsistence at risk				Subsistence assured	
	Owners	Owners	Croppers[a]	Croppers	Owners	Croppers
Farm income	−*[b]	−*	−	−	+*	+*
Age	+*	+*	+	+	−*	−
Family size	+	+*	−	+	+	+
Gambler dummy	+	+	+*	−*	+	+
Risk1[c]	+*	na	+*	na	na	na
Risk2[c]	na[d]	+*	na	+*	+*	+*

[a] 'Croppers' denotes sharecroppers.
[b] * denotes statistical significance at atleast the 5% level.
[c] Risk1 and Risk2 are the two alternative risk variables.
[d] 'na' denotes variable 'not applicable' for that regression.

Source: Based on Dillon and Scandizzo (1978, Table 6, p. 433).

off-farm income, a progressive farmer dummy (= 1 for a progressive farmer and 0 otherwise), luck (measured as an index of previous wins and losses in the games being played), net transfers received, age, women farmers' dummy (= 1 for women farmers and 0 otherwise), number of working age adults, net area rented, and a gambler dummy (= 1 if the individual gambles and 0 otherwise). The regressand was *ln S*, where *S* is partial risk aversion. Rather few of the results are significant, or even consistent. Out of the relatively consistent results, the variables wealth, education, off-farm income, progressive farmer dummy, net transfers received and luck are 'mostly' (i.e. in atleast five of the six regressions reported) negatively related to risk aversion. That is, a higher level of any of these regressors is associated with a lower level of risk aversion.

The above results may be subject to the criticism, amongst others, that some of the regressors are in fact endogenous. To account for possible endogeneity bias, Binswanger (1981) estimated a three-equation system where wealth and education were first estimated as functions of risk aversion (with wealth now redefined in net terms). Risk aversion was then

Table 2.6 Risk preferences and socioeconomic characteristics[a]

Dependent variable: *ln S*, where *S* is constant partial risk aversion.

| | Panel A | | | | | | Panel B |
| | Rs[a] 0.5 game | | Rs 5 game | | Rs 50 game | Rs 500 game | Rs 5 game |
Regressor	No. 2	No. 5	No. 7	No. 9			No. 7
Wealth	-*b	-	-	-*	+	-	-
Education	+	-	-*	-	-	-	-
Off-farm Income	+	-	-*	-	-	-*	na
Progressiveness dummy	-	-*	-*	+	-	-	na
Luck	-	-*	-*	-*	-*	-*	-
Net transfers received	-	-*	-*	-	-	+	na
Age	+	+	+	+*	-	-	+
Women dummy	+	+*	+	-	-	-	+
No. of adults	+	-	+	+	+	+	na
Land rented	-	-*	-	+	+	+	na
Gambler dummy	-	-	+	-	-	+	na
Caste rank	na[c]	na	na	na	na	na	+

[a] Rs denotes 'Rupees'.
[b] * denotes significance at atleast the 10% level.
[c] 'na' denotes variable 'not applicable' for that regression.

Source: Panel A — based on Binswanger (1980, Table 6, p. 403); Panel B — based on Binswanger (1981, Table 2, p. 879).

estimated as a function of (predicted) net assets, (predicted) education, age, women dummy, caste rank and luck (Table 2.6, panel B). Again, most of the coefficients are insignificant although wealth, education and luck are still found to be negatively related to risk aversion.

Walker (1981) estimated regressions similar to those of Binswanger (1980). The regressors employed were age, education, assets, type of tenure

Table 2.7 Risk preferences and socioeconomic characteristics

Regressand for method (iii): ln S (S is constant partial risk aversion)
Regressand for method (ii): Risk premium.

Regressor	Elicitation method (iii)		Elicitation method (ii)	
	Initial games	Last 6 games	On gains	On losses
Age	+	+* a	–	–
Education	–*	–*	–	–
Assets	+	–	–*	–
Tenure type	–	–	+	–
Off-farm income	–	–*	+	–
No. of adults	–	–	+	+
Luck	–	–	na b	na
Adopter dummy	+*	+*	+*	+
Game type dummy	–	na	na	na
Gambler dummy	–	+	–*	–
Game 5C c dummy	+*	+*	na	na
Game 10C dummy	+*	+	na	na
Game 50C dummy	+*	na	na	na

a * denotes significance at atleast the 10% level.
b 'na' denotes variable 'not applicable' for that regression.
c C denotes the currency 'Colon'.

Source: Based on Walker (1981, Table 3, p. 76).

(= 1 for fixed cash renter and 0 for owner-operator), off-farm income, number of working age adults, luck, adopter dummy (= 1 for the village which adopted the hybrid varieties and 0 for the village which did not), type-of-game dummy (= 1 for games with hypothetical payoffs and 0 for games with real payoffs), gambler dummy (= 1 if the respondent bought a lottery ticket in the 'previous year' and 0 otherwise), and size-of-game dummies for the 5, 10 and 50 colon games. The regressand was risk premium for the games with hypothetical payoffs, and *ln S* (as in Binswanger) for games with real payoffs. The results are fairly similar to those in Binswanger's study (Table 2.7). Few coefficients are statistically significant. We find variables wealth, education and off-farm income to be

Table 2.8 Risk preferences and socioeconomic characteristics

Dependent variable in regression 1: Proportional insurance premium
Dependent variable in regression 2: Constant partial risk aversion

Regressor	Regression 1	Regression 2
Std. deviation price	−*	+
Std. deviation yield	−*	−
Age	+	+
Multiple cropping	+*	+*
Farm size	−*	−*
Nonland assets	+*	+
Mathematical ability	+*	+*
Abstract ability	−	−

* denotes significance at atleast the 10% level.

Source: Based on Grisley and Kellogg (1987, Table 5, p. 139).

negatively related to risk aversion, as expected. The game-size dummy variables confirm the earlier finding that risk aversion increases with the stakes involved. Similarly, Grisley and Kellogg (1987) related risk aversion to the standard deviations of rice price and yield, age, multiple cropping dummy (= 1 for a single crop and 0 otherwise), farm size, nonland assets, mathematical ability and abstract ability (Table 2.8). The regressands were, alternatively, the proportional insurance premium and partial risk aversion. The regression is misspecified in that multiple cropping depends upon risk attitudes, not vice versa. Risk aversion is found to decrease significantly with farm size.

Moscardi and de Janvry (1977) used discriminant analysis to gauge the association between risk aversion and the variables age, education, family size, off-farm income, area operated and institutional access (proxied by a dummy variable equal to 1 if the farmer was part of a 'solidarity group' and 0 otherwise). The farmers were divided into three groups on the basis of the risk aversion parameter. The hypothesis of an association between risk aversion and the above-mentioned variables would be accepted if the discriminant function estimated assigned the farm household to the same group as did the risk aversion parameter. The analysis revealed a strong relationship between risk aversion and the land variable (the main form of

Table 2.9 Risk preferences and socioeconomic characteristics

Panel A: Dependent variable — Risk aversion measure based on
Kataoka's safety-first rule

Regressor	Coefficient sign
Age	+
Education	–
Family size	–
Land operated	–*
Off-farm income	–*
Institutional access dummy	–*

Panel B: Dependent variable — Risk aversion measure based on Roy's
safety-first rule

Regressor	Sylhet		Pabna		Faridpur		Mymensingh	
	R[a]	C[a]	R	C	R	C	R	C
Age	–	+	–*[b]	–	–	–	–*	–
Family size	+*	+*	+	+	+	+*	+*	+*
Education	–	–	+	–	+	–	–	–
Farm size	–*	–*	+	–	–	–*	–*	–*
Off-farm income	–*	–	–*	–*	–*	–*	+	–
Assets	+	+	+	+	+	+	–	–

[a] R denotes 'recorded data', and C 'computed data'.
[b] * denotes significance at atleast the 10% level.

Source: Panel A — based on Moscardi and de Janvry (1977, Table 5, p. 716); Panel B — based on Shahabuddin *et.al.* (1986, Table 2, p. 127).

holding wealth), off-farm income and the institutional access variable. This finding was supported by subsequent regression analysis, which revealed risk aversion to be significantly negatively related to off-farm income, land operated and the institutional access variable (Table 2.9, panel A).

Shahabuddin *et.al.* (1986) regressed risk aversion on age, family size,

Table 2.10 Risk preferences and socioeconomic characteristics

Panel A: Dependent variable — Coefficient of absolute risk aversion.
Regressor

Age	$-$* a
Education	$-$*
Land owned (%)	$+$*
Education sqd.	$+$*
Age x Education	$+$*
Education x land owned (%)	$-$*

Panel B: Elasticities of Constant Partial Risk Aversion

	Pastoral zone		Wheat–sheep zone		High rainfall zone	
Regressor	NLS[b]	3SLS[c]	NLS	3SLS	NLS	3SLS
Wealth	$-$*	$-$*	$-$*	$-$*	$-$*	$-$*
Income	$+$*	$+$	$+$*	$+$*	$+$*	$+$*

[a] * denotes significance at atleast the 10% level.

[b] NLS denotes nonlinear least squares.

[c] 3SLS denotes 3-stage least squares.

Source: Panel A — based on Halter and Mason (1978, Table 2, p. 105); Panel B — based on Bardsley and Harris (1987, Table 2, pp. 123-124).

education, farm size, off-farm income and the value of household assets. Regressions were run for two alternative estimates of the risk attitude measure (based on the 'reported' minimum consumption needs of the farm households and their 'computed' minimum consumption needs), for each of the four districts surveyed (Table 2.9, panel B). Risk aversion is found to be consistently positively related to family size, and is often significant. On the other hand, it is mostly negatively related to both farm size and off-farm income, and is often significant. Their specification is likely to be misspecified as it includes both farm size and value of assets as regressors. Since land is the overwhelmingly important asset in the rural setup, these two variables are likely to be strongly collinear; so that the (mostly) negative coefficient of the farm size variable is probably picking up the effect of the assets variable (and also making the latter insignificant). For this reason, we shall discount the results from this study, atleast as far as the wealth variable is concerned.

Halter and Mason (1978) regressed the coefficient of absolute risk aversion on age, education, percent of land owned, education squared, (age times education) and (education times percent land owned). Their results, Table 2.10, panel A, reveal age and education to be negatively related to risk aversion, and the percent of land owned (which may be interpreted as a 'tenancy variable') to be positively related. All relationships are found to be statistically significant. Although Bardsley and Harris (1987) did not include various socioeconomic variables in their model, their model did provide estimates of the elasticity of (constant) partial risk aversion with respect to income and wealth (Table 2.10, panel B). Risk aversion is found to have a significantly negative relation with wealth and a significantly positive relation with income. Moreover, this is consistently true of all the three Australian regions considered.

Bond and Wonder (1980) conduct chi-squared 'contingency tests' for the association of risk premium with the variables age, net worth, off-farm income, climatic zone and 'property type'(i.e. type of activity − beef dominant, sheep dominant etc.). Only off-farm income and 'property type' are found to be statistically significant, and that too under some situations. However, the direction of these relationships is not explored. Note that the statistical significance is tested at the 5% level. We would have liked to know the results using the 10% critical values, in order to conform with the significance criterion that we have used for evaluating the other studies. Nor was it possible for us to work out these critical values since the degrees of freedom vary between cells and these figures are not provided in the paper. Finally, Wilson and Eidman (1983) conduct a discriminant analysis to explore the relationship between risk aversion and net disposable income, age, education, debt ratio (i.e. total liabilities as a ratio of total assets), net worth, scale of operation (i.e. pounds of pigs produced), and the degree of specialisation (i.e. percentage of the enterprise which contributes most to total sales). Based on the estimated discriminant function, they find risk aversion to be negatively related to net disposable income, age and education. Although this relationship is also found to be negative for the debt and scale variables, it probably implies that a higher risk preference (lower risk aversion) manifests itself in terms of higher indebtedness and a larger scale of operations. Risk aversion is positively related to both the degree of specialisation and net worth. The former stands to reason, since the greater the proportion of total sales that come from a single enterprise the greater the aversion to risk. The latter, however, is inexplicable. Note, that the wealth and debt variables are likely to be inversely correlated given the way they are defined. So that when wealth increases the debt ratio declines. But a lower debt ratio is probably a manifestation of higher risk aversion, making for a positive relation between risk aversion and wealth. This apparently contrary result should therefore be discounted.

Some Generalisations

At one level it is somewhat difficult to generalise on the basis of the results discussed above because the different studies often employed different measures of risk aversion, defined a given regressor (for instance, wealth) differently, included different sets of explanatory variables in their empirical analyses, and sometimes used different estimation procedures to study the association between the variables. At another level, however, if despite these differences we can observe consistent relationships between risk aversion and certain socioeconomic characteristics, this may well indicate the robustness of these relationships. Before we proceed to do this, we must enter the caveat that running regressions of risk aversion on various socioeconomic characteristics (which is what most studies have done) is probably not the best way of trying to discern patterns of association between them. Many of the regressors used are probably not exogenous, as indeed is recognized in Binswanger (1981). While we cannot put much faith in the 'significant' results so obtained, at the same time we should also allow for the possibility that the 'insignificant' results obtained could also be due to the improper estimation procedures used. In sum, therefore, we can accept the existing results tentatively until more information becomes available.

The results discussed above permit us to make the following three propositions:

Propostion A1 Risk aversion is negatively related to a farmer's wealth.

A larger asset base probably implies a larger capacity to bear risks not only because it implies a larger savings fund to fall back upon and a smaller probability of falling below the subsistence level, but also because it may be used as collateral for raising credit when necessary. Given that land is often the major asset in rural economies, this would imply that large farmers are probably less risk averse than small farmers.

Proposition A2 Risk aversion is negatively related to the education levels of farmers.

Insofar as schooling enables a better evaluation of the available information, it probably serves to lessen the perception of risk and hence lowers risk aversion. Further, if education levels and wealth were positively related, this would strengthen the possibility mentioned in the previous paragraph, that large farmers may be relatively less risk averse. It is pertinent that although some researchers find little association between wealth and literacy (e.g. Dreze and Sen, 1995), we must distinguish between the definitions of education and literacy employed in the different studies. While the former relates to formal schooling, the latter relates to some *ad hoc* measures such as the number of characters (of a particular language) that a respondent knows, whether he can sign his name, whether he can read a letter etc.; so that 'education' would subsume 'literacy' but not vice versa. From the viewpoint of taking 'significant decisions', such literacy is probably irrelevant.

Proposition A3 Risk aversion is negatively related to off-farm income.

Off-farm income probably allows the hedging of perceived risks from self-cultivation, and hence lowers risk aversion. Insofar as small farmers supply more off-farm labour than large farmers and have relatively larger off-farm incomes, this factor would counter (though probably not overwhelm), the effects of the wealth and education variables on the risk aversion of small farmers. Considering the effect of all three variables (i.e. wealth, education and off-farm income), in other words, we would still expect large farmers to be relatively less risk averse than small farmers.

All the three relationships noted above were found to be statistically significant in a 'large enough' number of cases to allow us to make the above inferences with a reasonable degree of confidence. While these generalisations may not be accepted as 'facts', they may be treated as working hypotheses. This was not quite true of the other socioeconomic variables, where the relationships were not even consistently negative or positive, leave alone statistically significant.

3 The Survey Sample and its Characteristic Features

Introduction

In *The Adventure of the Copper Beeches*, at one juncture Dr. Watson recounts that '... Holmes ... sat ... for half an hour on end, with knitted brow and an abstracted air, but he swept the matter away with a wave of his hand when I mentioned it. Data! Data! Data!, he cried impatiently, I can't make bricks without clay'. And indeed one can't. So also the estimation of the household decision-theoretic models developed in the previous chapter require, ideally, data collected at the level of rural households. Further, the data set needs to be sufficiently rich in information if we are to have available the numerous regressors that we have discussed in relation to the models derived above. While very large household level cross-section data sets are available — for instance, the National Sample Survey data collected for rural households in India every few years — these do not provide information on most of the variables of interest to us. This is amply brought out by Bardhan (1984a), as noted in the introductory chapter. Moreover, the power of a data set would be enhanced if it provided information on a set of households not just for a single year, but also over a period of time. This would become prohibitively costly if the number of households sampled were very large, as it is in the National Sample Surveys where the sample sizes are usually several thousand units. At the same time, if the number of households is too small, not only does that raise statistical problems relating to insufficient degrees of freedom but also raises doubts about the general applicability of the results obtained. Luckily, we had at our disposal a powerful household level data set collected by the International Crops Research Institute for the Semi-Arid Tropics (ICRISAT), located in Hyderabad (India), as part of its village level studies. Specific characteristics of the sample households are discussed in the immediately following section. Although data on most of the variables of interest are provided by the data set, some variables — namely, the risk variables and the wage rate — need to be computed. This is taken up in the subsequent two sections. But for the present, we proceed

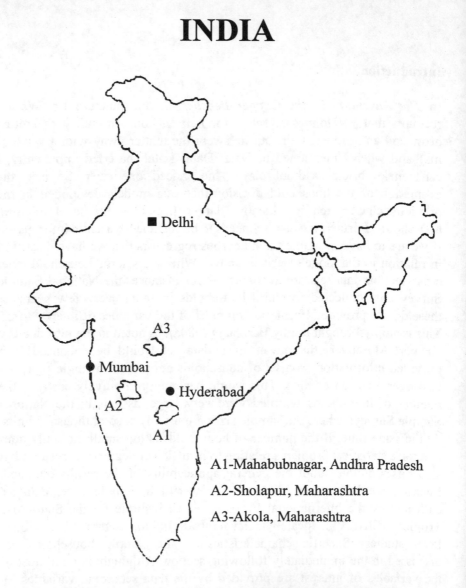

INDIA

A1-Mahabubnagar, Andhra Pradesh

A2-Sholapur, Maharashtra

A3-Akola, Maharashtra

**Figure 3.1 The three sample villages are located in the districts
shown in this map — Aurepalle in district
Mahabubnagar (A1), Shirapur in district Sholapur (A2)
and Kanzara in district Akola (A3)**

with a discussion of the general features of the data set.

The data set pertains to three villages — Aurepalle, Shirapur and Kanzara — situated in diverse agroclimatic zones in the Indian semi-arid tropics. These three villages are located in the 'districts' shown in Figure 3.1: Aurepalle in district Mahabubnagar (A1), Shirapur in district Sholapur (A2) and Kanzara in district Akola (A3).[1] District Mahabubnagar is in the Indian state of Andhra Pradesh, and districts Sholapur and Akola are in the state of Maharashtra. The data were collected for a time period of 10 agricultural years from 1975-76 to 1984-85.[2] In order to truly represent the rural setting, villages participating in special programmes, receiving extraordinary resource transfers (such as remittances), or located near towns and highways, were not selected. Further, the villages were chosen so as to be representative of the typical characteristics of the corresponding 'taluka', which, in turn, had been chosen as representative of the corresponding district.[3] The districts were purposively selected to represent the diverse agroclimatic and edaphic characteristics of the Indian semi-arid tropics. To ensure the representativeness of the sample unit at each stage of the sampling process, a large number of relevant characteristics were considered such as the density of population, the extent of literacy, the densities of cultivators, agricultural labourers, cattle etc., area irrigated, percentage share of important crops and so on.[4] Therefore, the conclusions holding for these regions may quite justifiably be taken to apply to large tracts of the Indian semi-arid tropics.

Aurepalle is characteristic of regions with alfisol soils, and low and uncertain rainfall. Shirapur is representative of regions with medium to deep vertisol soils, coupled with low and uncertain rainfall. Kanzara is typical of medium vertisols with relatively high and assured rainfall. The average annual rainfall was about 635mm in Aurepalle, about 643mm in Shirapur and about 872mm in Kanzara over the 10 year sample period. The associated standard deviations were 252mm, 227mm and 206mm, respectively. More than 90% of the cultivated area in Aurepalle and Kanzara was planted during the rainy season, which stretched from mid-June to mid-October. In Shirapur, the bulk of the cultivated area was sown during the post-rainy season only in 'dry' years, with this proportion being only about 50% in normal years.[5] Therefore, it would be instructive to look at the rainfall patterns in the period June to September with reference to the sowing of both rainy season crops as well as post-rainy season crops sowed in residual moisture. From Table 3.1 we find, that in Aurepalle, the actual rainfall in the month of June was less than three-fourths of the 10-year average for June in 4 out of 10 years. For the months of July, August and

Table 3.1 Rainfall patterns during July-September

	Rainfall averages[a]			No. of deficit years[b]		
	Aurepalle	Shirapur	Kanzara	Aurepalle	Shirapur	Kanzara
June	78.8	73.5	157.3	4	2	3
July	104.6	105.4	215.0	3	6	2
Aug.	133.6	98.9	214.9	4	4	3
Sep.	165.7	195.4	137.6	4	5	4

[a] Averages are for rainfall in a specific month over the entire period 1975-76/84-85.

[b] A 'deficit' year was defined as one in which the actual rainfall in a specific month was less than or equal to three-fourths of the 10-year average for that month.

September, the rainfall was 'deficit' in the above sense in 3, 4 and 4 years out of 10, respectively. Similarly, for Shirapur, the number of deficit years ranged between 2 out of 10 for June and 6 out of 10 for July; while for Kanzara they ranged between 2 out of 10 for July and 4 out of 10 for September. Thus, in the case of all three villages there were several years when the crops faced substantial stress on account of insufficient moisture at sowing time, affecting their prospects negatively. Add to this the deleterious effects of an uneven *distribution* of rainfall over the crop seasons. As one would expect, farmers responded to these events '... by changing crops or by fallowing land' (Walker and Ryan, 1990, p. 34). The implications of all these effects and counter-effects, ceteris paribus, would be to lessen the *potential* employment (of family and/or hired labour) over the crop cycle, thereby inducing the farmers to sell their labour in the off-farm casual labour market to hedge against the production risks.

In each of these villages, 40 households were randomly picked — 10 from amongst the agricultural labour households, or those operating less than 0.2 hectares of land, and 10 each from the groups of small, medium and large farmers. The land size classes defining these groups are given in Table 3.2. On account of variations in the land-man ratios, the size of operational landholdings and land productivity differences between the sample villages, it was not desirable to have uniform land size classes for all villages. Evidently, if the natural resources endowments in one village are more productive than those in another, a 'small' farmer in the former

Table 3.2 Farm size classification[*]

Units: Hectares

Village	Small farms	Medium farms	Large farms
Aurepalle	0.20 ≤ 2.50	2.51 ≤ 5.26	> 5.26
Shirapur	0.20 ≤ 2.50	2.51 ≤ 5.87	> 5.87
Kanzara	0.20 ≤ 2.26	2.27 ≤ 5.59	> 5.59

[*] The farm size classification is based on operational holding size.

Source: Based on Table 3, Singh *et.al.* (1985).

village would not exactly correspond to a 'small' farmer in the latter; hence the need to allow for such differences in determining land-size classes.

The cultivator households constituted the predominant proportion of all the households in the villages (Table 3.3), as is typical of under-developed agriculture in general. Thus, 68% of all the households in Aurepalle, 62% of the households in Shirapur and 64% of the households in Kanzara were cultivator households. The landless or agricultural labour households, though only about half as numerous, still accounted for substantial proportions of the households in these villages. Thus, 30% of the households in Aurepalle, 32% of the households in Shirapur and 32% of the households in Kanzara were landless households. In other words, the cultivator and labour households together accounted for over 96% of the households in these villages, the remainder comprising artisans, shopkeepers etc..

There were several reasons why many of the cultivator and labour households originally sampled could not be included in the specific sample that we utilised for our empirical exercises. Some households which were part of the study to begin with moved away from the mandate villages sometime during the course of the study. While these households were replaced with other randomly selected households in the same villages, we preferred to drop such households from our sample. The reason for this was the fact that such a replacement procedure would vitiate the panel nature of our sample. Thus, observing these households over the full 10 year period, one would notice abrupt changes in such variables of interest as the number of working members in the family, the number of children, the ages of the family members etc. And we would know that these changes had occurred not on account of the 'normal growth processes' in the family

Table 3.3 Distribution of households by primary occupation

Village	Landless households	Cultivator households	Others[a]	Total
Aurepalle	146 (30)[b]	322 (68)	8 (2)	476 (100)
Shirapur	97 (32)	183 (62)	17 (6)	297 (100)
Kanzara	54 (32)	109 (64)	6 (4)	169 (100)

[a] The 'others' category includes artisans, shopkeepers etc.
[b] The figures in parentheses are percentages.

Source: Based on Table 2, Singh *et.al.* (1985).

and the village economy, but because of extraneous causes — namely, that the migrant household had been substituted by another. While a cross section-time series would suffice if we were exploring some aggregate relationships (say, the aggregate consumption function), panel data is much more appropriate for analysing household level decision-making as one would be surer of the *sources of change* over time. Secondly, while information for some of the households was available for the beginning and ending years of the study, it was not available for the interim because they had migrated temporarily. Finally, some households had to be excluded because data on all the variables of interest was not available in their case for various reasons, although they had been resident in the village for the entire length of the study. Consequently, we were left with a total of 23 landless and 53 (owner) cultivator households in the three villages for which all the data were available for the entire 10 year period 1975-76/84-85. Of the 23 landless households in our sample, 8 were resident in Aurepalle, 6 in Shirapur and 9 in Kanzara. Of the 53 cultivator households, 18 were resident in Aurepalle, 13 in Shirapur and 22 in Kanzara. This meant that the total number of observations available was fairly large, 230 for the landless households and 530 for the cultivator households.

Principal Features of the Sample Units

At this stage, it might be instructive to look at some of the principal characteristics of our sample. Table 3.4 presents the (arithmetic) means and

Table 3.4 Central tendencies of some variables

Variable[a]	Mean[b] (Standard deviation): Landless households							
	Total		Aurepalle		Shirapur		Kanzara	
AGE	51.2	(10.3)	53.8	(10.1)	50.1	(7.8)	49.3	(13.3)
EDU	0.7	(1.4)	0.0	(0.0)	1.3	(1.9)	0.5	(1.1)
WRKMEM	2.6	(1.5)	2.6	(1.4)	3.0	(1.5)	1.9	(1.3)
DEPMEM	2.2	(1.5)	2.3	(1.4)	2.2	(1.5)	2.2	(1.7)
CASTE	4.4	(2.2)	5.8	(1.4)	4.3	(2.6)	2.8	(1.5)
NLASS	26.2	(23.7)	22.2	(0.7)	30.3	(29.0)	25.5	(21.1)
OWNFARM	29.5	(91.8)	14.9	(15.1)	52.1	(142.4)	15.0	(22.9)
OFFARM	189.0	(210.6)	121.0	(137.7)	189.0	(189.0)	279.7	(279.6)
IUE	111.6	(142.3)	87.1	(67.1)	106.0	(111.0)	152.8	(226.9)
WR	3.7	(1.7)	2.8	(1.3)	4.2	(2.1)	3.9	(1.3)

Variable	Mean (Standard deviation): Cultivator households							
	Total		Aurepalle		Shirapur		Kanzara	
AGE	49.7	(11.4)	55.1	(11.9)	51.1	(8.9)	44.4	(9.9)
EDU	2.5	(3.6)	1.8	(2.9)	1.3	(1.9)	3.8	(4.4)
WRKMEM	3.8	(1.9)	3.1	(1.5)	4.2	(2.1)	4.1	(2.0)
DEPMEM	3.0	(1.9)	2.7	(1.6)	2.7	(1.7)	3.5	(2.2)
CASTE	2.9	(1.9)	3.7	(2.1)	2.5	(2.0)	2.6	(1.6)
NLASS	115.6	(109.1)	126.8	(133.9)	98.9	(52.7)	116.2	(110.4)
GCA	16.6	(15.8)	12.5	(10.3)	19.9	(13.6)	18.1	(19.7)
PAIRR	10.8	(18.2)	14.7	(19.6)	14.0	(22.2)	5.6	(12.3)
INEXP	16.1	(24.4)	15.5	(22.1)	14.5	(25.4)	17.5	(25.6)
LVAL	24.2	(14.6)	21.2	(12.7)	35.4	(15.9)	20.1	(11.4)
OWNFARM	100.4	(117.9)	82.3	(79.8)	103.2	(125.7)	113.5	(136.4)
OFFARM	99.9	(170.9)	80.3	(167.8)	103.1	(182.0)	114.0	(165.8)
IUE	58.0	(99.3)	48.8	(80.5)	48.4	(75.9)	71.2	(121.9)
WR	2.9	(2.7)	1.6	(1.9)	4.7	(3.3)	3.0	(2.4)

[a] The units of measurement are: AGE (years), EDU (years), WRKMEM (number), DEPMEM (number), CASTE (rank), NLASS (Rs. '00), GCA (acres), PAIRR (percentage), INEXP (Rs. '00), LVAL (Rs. '00), OWNFARM (days), OFFARM (days), IUE (days), WR (Rs. per day).

[b] 'Mean' refers to the arithmetic mean.

standard deviations for different variables relating to the cultivator and landless labour households. The averages have been estimated for the entire 10 year period from 1975-76 to 1984-85. We shall first discuss the human capital variables and household characteristics that are common to both groups of households, and then consider those that pertain to the cultivator households only. Finally, we shall take a look at the labour allocation patterns of both sets of households.

The average age of the household head (AGE) is about 51.1 years for the landless households and 49.7 years for the cultivator households, with a standard deviation of only a little over 10 years in both cases. This would suggest that a large percentage of the decision makers were probably well-experienced. Both groups of households are fairly illiterate, having less than three years of formal education (EDU). However, with less than a year's education the group of landless households appears to be definitely less educated than the cultivator households who spent about 2.5 years in school. At such low levels of formal education, it becomes difficult to gauge *a priori* whether this variable would successfully capture the effects that it is supposed to − namely, the garnering of nontraditional skills which gives rise to higher monetary expectations on the one hand and serves to increase a worker's on-farm productivity by increasing his all-round skills, on the other. An alternative measure, however, is not very obvious. The number of prime age working members (WRKMEM) in landless labour households averages 2.6 as against 3.8 for the cultivator households. Again, the number of dependents (DEPMEM) in landless households (2.2) is less than that in cultivator households (3.0). Prime age workers were defined as all those between the ages of 15 and 55 years, inclusive. The category of dependents comprised the residual (which may be further sub-divided into the young dependents or those less than 15, and elderly dependents or those over 55 years of age). Note that these categories are of an *a priori* nature; the actual number of workers and dependents is decided *a posteriori*. Putting together the above two variables, we find that cultivator households have substantially larger families than landless labour households, partially indicating their relatively superior economic status. Our data set provides us with three alternative measures of the households' 'caste' status − those due to V. Doherty, J. Behrman and J. Ryan. Doherty's index is based on the households' social, economic and religious status in the village, with a somewhat larger weight placed on the religious rank. The index proposed by Behrman takes note of the fact that different castes appear with different frequencies in a given population. His index, therefore, computes the rank ordering of castes in

Table 3.5 Spearman's rank correlations between alternative caste measures

	Landless and Cultivator Households		
	Casted[a]	Casteb[b]	Caster[c]
Casted	1.00	-0.91	0.96
Casteb	–	1.00	-0.86
Caster	–	–	1.00

	Landless Households		
	Casted	Casteb	Caster
Casted	1.00	-0.94	0.90
Casteb	–	1.00	-0.85
Caster	–	–	1.00

	Cultivator Households		
	Casted	Casteb	Caster
Casted	1.00	-0.87	0.98
Casteb	–	1.00	-0.84
Caster	–	–	1.00

[a] 'Casted' refers to the caste index due to V. Doherty.
[b] 'Caster' refers to the caste indices due to J. Behrman.
[c] 'Caster' refers to the caste indices due to J. Ryan.

the sample by adjusting for the different relative frequencies of the different groups. The third index, that due to Ryan, is based on the occupational and socioeconomic condition of the households (Singh *et.al.*, 1985). A simple correlation analysis using Spearman's rank correlation coefficients (Table 3.5) shows that there is little to gain in statistical terms from preferring any particular index over the others. We select Doherty's index (CASTE) because it is relatively comprehensive as to the underlying factors determining the overall status of a household. This index ranks all the 'castes' between 1 and 7, with 1 representing the highest caste and 7 the lowest. The mean caste index for the group of landless households works out to about 4.4, whereas for the cultivator households it stands predictably

Table 3.6 F-tests[a] for the difference of variable means across villages

Variable	Landless households F-statistic[b]	(D.o.f)[c]	Cultivator households F-statistic[b]	(D.o.f)
AGE	0.26	(2, 227)[d]	2.92	(2, 527)[e]
EDU	50.79	(2, 227)	46.56	(2, 527)
WRKMEM	5.58	(2, 227)	5.02	(2, 527)
DEPMEM	0.03	(2, 227)	5.97	(2, 527)
CASTE	17.02	(2, 227)	16.11	(2, 527)
NLASS	1.97	(2, 227)	2.97	(2, 527)
GCA	na[f]	na	10.29	(2, 527)
PAIRR	na	na	30.41	(2, 527)
INEXP	na	na	1.75	(2, 527)
LVAL	na	na	34.18	(2, 527)
OFFARM	34.81	(2, 227)	2.23	(2, 527)
OWNFARM	11.32	(2, 227)	2.28	(2, 527)
IUE	7.16	(2, 227)	5.14	(2, 527)
WR	3.53	(2, 227)	17.36	(2, 527)

[a] The null hypothesis is that of equal means for a given variable across all three sample villages.

[b] The test statistic is computed as $F = (SSB/K-1)/(SSW/N-K)$, where SSB is 'between group sum of squares', SSW is 'within group sum of squares', K is the number of means being compared (three in this case), and $N = \sum n_k$ (n_k being the number of observations on the variable in question for the kth village).

[c] 'D.o.f' denotes 'degrees of freedom'.

[d] The critical values for $F(2, 227)$ are 3.009 and 4.704 at the 5% and 1% levels of significance, respectively.

[e] The critical values for $F(2, 527)$ are 2.996 and 4.606 at the 5% and 1% levels of significance, respectively.

[f] 'na' denotes 'not applicable'.

lower at 2.9, indicating a relatively higher all-round status for the latter. Nonland assets (NLASS) — comprising livestock, implements and buildings — averaged a meagre Rs. 2620 for the landless households, and a more substantial Rs. 11555 for the cultivator households. As expected, the cultivator households are better off.

We conducted F-tests to test whether the variable means were significantly different across villages for each of the two occupation groups, as well as across the two groups themselves. Under the null hypothesis of equal means for a given variable across all three villages, the test statistic was computed as $F = (SSB/K-1)/(SSW/N-K)$ where SSB is 'between group sum of squares', SSW is 'within group sum of squares', K is the number of means being compared (three in this case), and $N = \sum n_k$ where n_k is the number of observations on the variable of interest for the kth village. (For comparisons across the occupational or household categories, K would equal two and n_k would be the number of observations on the variable of interest for the kth group). Under the null hypothesis, the test statistic has an F-distribution with $(K-1, N-K)$ degrees of freedom. For the group of landless labour households, the null hypothesis of equal variable means across the villages of Aurepalle, Shirapur and Kanzara was rejected only for the variables education, prime age workers and caste (Table 3.6). For the group of cultivator households, the means were found to be significantly different across the villages in the case of education, prime age workers, number of dependents and caste (Table 3.6). Finally, a comparison of all the landless households with all the cultivator households revealed that the null hypothesis of equal means was strongly rejected in the case of education, number of prime age working members, number of dependents, nonland assets and caste (Table 3.7).

Let us now consider the variables that exclusively relate to the cultivator households (see Table 3.4 again). The cultivated or gross cropped area (GCA) averages about 16.6 acres. While this figure does not illumine us about the cropping intensity, the incidence of multiple cropping is likely to be rather low since only a very small percentage of this area is irrigated. Thus, the irrigated area amounts to a paltry average of a trifle over two acres. The percentage area irrigated (PAIRR) averaged only 10.8%, ranging from 5.6% for Kanzara to 14.7% for Aurepalle. The use of modern inputs was rather small, as indicated by the total input expenditure on fertilizer, machinery and manures (INEXP) of only about Rs. 1600. The average land value (LVAL) was about Rs. 2400 per acre, indicating rather low productivity. The means for all the variables except input expenditure were significantly different across the sample villages (Table 3.6).

Looking at the labour allocation patterns for landless households, we find that they supply about 189 (standard eight hour) days in off-farm work (OFFARM) as against only some 30 days in own-farm work (OWNFARM). This makes sense since landless labour households are those

Table 3.7 F-tests[a] for the difference of variable means across occupational groups

Variable	F-statistic[b]	(D.o.f)[c]
AGE	1.99	(1, 758)[d]
EDU	195.55	(1, 758)
WRKMEM	163.86	(1, 758)
DEPMEM	25.93	(1, 758)
CASTE	109.52	(1, 758)
NLASS	299.05	(1, 758)
GCA	na[e]	(1, 758)
PAIRR	na	(1, 758)
LVAL	na	(1, 758)
OWNFARM	440.59	(1, 758)
OFFARM	70.76	(1, 758)
IUE	252.74	(1, 758)
WR	55.72	(1, 758)

[a] The null hypothesis is that of equal means for a given variable across the two occupational groups of landless and farm households.
[b] The F-statistic is calculated as in Table 3.6, except that k is now two, and n_k is the number of observations on the variable of interest for the kth group.
[c] 'D.o.f' denotes 'degrees of freedom'.
[d] The critical values for F(1, 758) are 3.842 and 6.635 at the 5% and 1% levels of significance, respectively.
[e] 'na' denotes 'not applicable'.

with operational holdings of less than 0.2 hectares (see Table 3.2), and hence have to earn their livelihoods in the labour market. In comparison, the cultivator households spend approximately 100 days both in off-farm and own-farm work. This is in consonance with the fact, that in addition to production on their own plots, these households have wage labour as an alternative source of livelihood. For the same reasons, landless households manifest a greater magnitude of involuntary unemployment (IUE), about 112 days, than do the cultivator households, about 58 days. The average daily wage rate (WR) earned by landless households (Rs. 3.7 per day) exceeds that earned by the cultivator households (Rs. 2.9 per day). As regards inter-village variations, the mean levels of all four of the above-mentioned variables differ significantly in the case of the landless households (Table 3.6). But for cultivator households, the differences are significant for only involuntary unemployment and the daily wage rate (Table 3.6). Considering the variation across the two groups of households (Table 3.7), the differences in the mean levels of each of these variables were highly significant, as one would expect. From the above observations it is apparent, that the households populating the semi-arid tracts are endowed with a rather small and low-productivity assets base, with some regions (villages) relatively luckier than others, and with the cultivator households somewhat better off than their landless counterparts. This is true not only of the physical (land and nonland) asset base, but of the human capital assets as well, which has obvious implications for the capacity of the farmers to exploit their resource base. All these factors interact to make for a fairly risk-prone production and employment environment.

Moments of the Net Revenue Distributions

For the rural household models developed in chapter 2 to be estimable, we need estimates of the production risks faced by the individual farm households. Since we require information on household-specific risks, and because all the households in a given village may be presumed to receive the same rainfall, capturing production risk in terms of rainfall variability would be inadequate. Second, depending on the individual households' asset endowments — the moisture-retention capacity of their soils, the proportion of their plots irrigated, the extent of application of fertilisers, pesticides and weedicides, the amount of credit they can command etc. — rainfall variability may be associated with different perceptions of risk for different households. Third, rainfall variability relates only to variability in the *quantity* of rainfall. Equally pertinent are factors such as rainfall *distribution*. In addition, other factors such as temperature/sunshine, the incidence of hail along with the rain etc., could also be important. Fourth, there could be certain interaction effects of poor or over-abundant rainfall. Thus, Walker and Ryan (1990) note that '... when the southwest monsoon is late, the scope for pest damage on sorghum is greatly enhanced ...' (p. 36), and again '[A]bundant and sustained rain in late September and early October precipitated a sharp rise in insect and disease infestation' (p. 49). In other words, 'rainfall variability' as conventionally measured is an inadequate measure of even 'rainfall risk', leave alone 'weather risk' and 'yield variability'. Fifth, even yield variability may be inappropriate, because production risks may arise on account of price variability as well (and prices may vary in a direction opposite to that of quantities or yields). Instead of trying to take account of all these myriad factors one by one, we represent production risk in terms of a relatively portmanteau variable — namely, net revenue variability.

For this purpose we need information about the moments of the distributions of net revenue for the individual farm households. Farm households, by definition, have crop husbandry as their major occupation. Animal husbandry was not an important source of income for our sample cultivators. In truth, the expectations of revenue are some beliefs in the minds of the farmers, formed on the basis of 'long' experience in the profession. To make this approach functional, however, we must translate these beliefs into some observable variables. To this end, we approximate expected net returns by the conditional expectation of actual net revenue. The underlying logic is, that just as the latter relates to a probabilistic situation, so does the former involve the use of (subjective) 'probabilities'. This allows us to jointly estimate the conditional expectation and variance of the net revenue distributions using an appropriate econometric model.

Note, however, that although we introduced production risk in terms of the multiplicative error term of the production function in the theoretical model in chapter 2, we cannot merely estimate a production function to derive the conditional moments of the revenue distribution. In other words a production function would not constitute the 'appropriate econometric model' that we refer to in the previous paragraph. First, a production function relates *output, not revenue*, to input use. Second, the regressors pertain to *input quantities, not input expenditure*. Therefore, the 'production function estimated by regressing revenue on input expenditure is not really the production function. Such a relation may seriously distort the input-output relation, yielding very inaccurate estimates of the errors. Third, estimating a single production function would amount to the assumption that the same technological relation between inputs and output holds for all the crops aggregated over. This is not generally true. Thus, the production function for sorghum, millets, rice, castor and cotton (the major crops grown in the sample villages) would differ from each other. Further, such a procedure would be all the more questionable since the cropping pattern is likely to differ over the years, entailing corresponding changes in the quantities of inputs used. Fourth, accounting for 'all' the major inputs into production often becomes impractical, so that only a few major ones such as labour, land, capital etc. are identified and many others are ignored. In fact, the production function literature reveals so many problems with its estimation that we preferred to eschew this approach (see Rudra, 1982, chapter 1; and the references therein).

As an alternative we choose the following way out for modelling the growth in total output/revenue over the sample period. Although agricultural output/revenue appears to be affected by a host of important factors over the course of the cropping season, this need not prevent us from hypothesizing an approximate relation based on *a priori* theoretical considerations. In so doing we shall use the terms 'output' and 'revenue' interchangeably. What we are concerned with are the outputs of the various crops grown by the farmers, but for purposes of aggregation we must deal in value or revenue terms.

It seems reasonable to argue that the (absolute or percentage) change in output is related to the preceding period's output (Dandekar, 1980). Then the appropriate functional form would be

$$\log q_t = \alpha + \beta t \tag{3.1}$$

The above function implies that $dq/dt = \beta q$, thereby vindicating our relational hypothesis. The idea here is to estimate the trend growth in revenue over the sample period. Deviations from this estimated trend may then be attributed to various factors underlying production risk. When we represent the movement in total output/revenue using the above relation, it does *not* imply that output is growing over time *on account of* time. It is well-recognised that the changes in output/revenue over time occur on account of changes in area cultivated, seed varieties used, labour, irrigation, fertilisers, pesticides/weedicides/insecticides, mechanisation, tenurial systems etc., and the weather. Let us express this relation as $q = G(X, W)$ where X is the vector of inputs and W the 'weather'. An acceptable representation of this relation is $ln\ q = A + Bln\ X + Cln\ W$, or $ln\ q = A + Bln\ X$ if we disregard the weather term as a random element, i.e. it would enter as an error term. Note that this specification is compatible with the production function specified in the theoretical model. Now if there is a trend movement in total output/revenue, and it *does* make sense to talk of such a trend, then this must be due to a trend in input use (given a random 'weather' term). Let the trend in inputs (over the sample period) be $X = ke^{b't}$. Then it is easy to show that the previous equation may be written as $ln\ q = \alpha + \beta t$, where $\alpha = A + Bln\ k$ and $\beta = Bb'$, which is none other than relation (3.1) hypothesized above. Thus, by using this relation we may circumvent estimating the production function.

Function (3.1) implies a constant rate of change of output over time. To allow for the possibility that the rate of change may itself be changing we may postulate the relation

$$\log q_t = \alpha + \beta t + \gamma t^2 \qquad (3.2)$$

which implies that $dq/dt = (\beta + 2\gamma t)q$, thereby incorporating our amended hypothesis. At this point we must emphasize that the dependent variable of interest is *net* revenue and not gross revenue. That it is the former and not the latter magnitude which is pertinent to the farmers' decision-making, should need no persuasion. But the problem is, that since the harvest may fail for many a reason, net revenue can be negative. Indeed, it sometimes is in our sample. For this reason we are precluded from estimating the models hypothesized above.[6] To circumvent this difficulty, we adopt the following line of approach. Note again that model (3.2) implies the first-order differential equation $dq/dt = (\beta + 2\gamma t)q$. Implicit in the use of derivatives is a continuous-time view of the world. On the other hand, if we were to treat time as a discrete variable, changes in q would be expressed in terms of differences rather than differentials. More explicitly, the change in q between any two time periods may then be expressed as $\Delta q/\Delta t$, where the operator 'Δ' represents discrete changes or differences. Further, when we are referring to changes in q between consecutive time periods, $\Delta t = 1$, so that the difference quotient $\Delta q/\Delta t$ may simply be written as Δq. Taking the cue from the first-order differential equation mentioned above, we may, alternatively, postulate the same relationship in terms of a first-order *difference* equation. Thus, we hypothesize that

$$\Delta q_t = q_t - q_{t-1} = f(q_{t-1}, t) \qquad (3.3)$$

which may be approximated by the linear relation

$$\Delta q_t = q_t - q_{t-1} = \delta_0 + \delta_{11} q_{t-1} + \delta_2 t$$

$$\Rightarrow q_t = \delta_0 + (1 + \delta_{11}) q_{t-1} + \delta_2 t$$

$$\Rightarrow q_t = \delta_0 + \delta_1 q_{t-1} + \delta_2 t \qquad \text{where } \delta_1 = (1 + \delta_{11}) \qquad (3.4)$$

Estimating an econometric model based on this functional relationship will give us joint estimates of the conditional moments of net revenue, which may be used to represent the effect of production risk.

While this specification may serve to capture the influence of factors in previous periods, current period output will also be affected by current period rainfall. Further, the households may try to mitigate the effect of the actual production risk that they face by drawing on their nonland assets (say, livestock). Analysing the ICRISAT data for 1976-77/81-82 Walker and Ryan (1990) state that '... we cannot show that mean livestock sales were significantly greater in shortfall years ...'. Note, however, that their sample period does not exactly overlap ours. Agarwal (1990) finds that farmers seldom sell or mortgage their assets unless there is a serious shortfall in their incomes (which is likely to be truer of semi-arid agriculture), but feels that the quantitative evidence is scanty. Overall, the evidence is weak and the possibility of this variable being significant cannot be ruled out. Thus, especially in the semi-arid regions, variations in output *may* also be related to variations in livestock. Therefore, we use 'current rainfall' and 'change in nonland assets' as additional regressors in our econometric specification.[7] Finally, specification of the error process would complete the specification of the statistical model, and also enable us to decide on the particular moments that would suffice to capture the risk distributions.

Making a careful assessment of the situation Walker and Subba Rao (1982) indicate, that the assumption of a normally distributed error process for the net returns distributions is probably a reasonable maintained hypothesis. In their study pertaining to five ICRISAT villages (of which three villages are the ones comprising our sample), albeit over the shorter time span 1975-76/1980-81, they explain net revenue variations in terms of farm management (or farmer), temporal (or cropping year) and spatial (or soil) effects for the different categories of cropping systems.[8] Using binary variable regression techniques, they find the latter two variables to be the most important. Analysing the estimated net revenue data, they conclude that '[A] normal distribution is probably a sufficiently close approximation to reality to describe the shape of net revenue distributions for most improved and some traditional cropping systems. Therefore, the assumption of normality ... may not be unduly restrictive' (p. 34). A traditional cropping system to which this statement relates is found in Aurepalle. As the authors explain '[A] diversity of components, and multiple sources of risk ... enforce normality on the net return distribution' (p. 26). Again, an improved cropping system to which the above statement refers is to be found in Kanzara. However, for other crop combinations in

Kanzara, and particularly in the village of Shirapur, the authors suggest that the net returns distribution is skewed to the right. An important factor tempering the above observation is, that the crop combinations considered to be 'common' or representative of a given village are merely the ones most frequently found in that village, i.e. the ones grown by the predominant *number* of farmers in that village. These cropping systems, however, are by no means dominant in those villages, occupying less than 50% of the cropped area on average in any cropping year. Unfortunately, the authors do not provide us with any figures on the importance of these cropping systems in terms of the *percentage of revenues* that they account for.[9] Walker and Subba Rao explain that this lack of predominance of any given crop combination in the sample villages may be attributed to diverse inter-cropping combinations and a heterogenous resource base. These very factors, as we saw above, were instrumental in imparting normality to the net returns distribution for Aurepalle. On the basis of the above arguments, we feel that the assumption of normally distributed net returns distributions in the sample villages may be a reasonable first approximation. Using this assumption, we get the estimation model

$$q_t = \delta_0 + \delta_1 q_{t-1} + \delta_2 t + \delta_3 R_t + \delta_4 \Delta \text{NLASS}_t + \eta_t \qquad (3.5)$$

where R_t is the current period rainfall, $\Delta NLASS_t$ is the change in nonland assets, η_t is the error term such that $\eta_t \sim N(\mu, \sigma^2)$, and the other variables are as defined before. We estimated model (3.5) to derive joint estimates of the conditional expectation of net revenue and the associated conditional standard deviation, for each of the farm households in the sample. The ratio of the latter to the former then gave us the coefficient of variation of net revenue (CVNR) for each of the households.

Estimation of Real Wage Rates

Since the data set provides wage rates only for those who actually supply labour, and since even the actual figures available should not be used directly for various reasons explained below, we conclude this chapter with the construction of the wage rate variable. In order to derive estimates of the expected real wage rate (ERWR), first of all we require data on the *actual wage rate* (WR, corresponding to w in the theoretical model), for 'each household-year' of our sample (i.e. for each household in each year of the sample period). However, the computation of the actual wage rate for off-farm work presented some difficulties, as it usually does in such studies. The data usually report the number of off-farm labour days worked by an individual, and the total wages earned for that work, as was the case with our data set. But since the dependent variable in analyses of labour supply pertains to the off-farm labour supplied, we cannot simply divide the wages earned from off-farm work (Rupees) by the number of (standard or eight hour) days worked, in order to arrive at the daily wage rate figures (Rupees/day). For one, this would cause measurement errors in the left-hand-side variable (labour days supplied), to be transmitted to the right-hand-side variable (the wage rate), the two being inversely related if the wage rate is measured in the above-mentioned manner. While measurement errors in the left-hand-side variable can be subsumed in the error term, those in the right-hand-side variable(s) would result in biased and inconsistent estimators (Judge *et.al.*, 1988). Secondly, the actual wage rate for some individuals may be zero in some periods, since they may not have supplied any off-farm work in those periods. At the same time these individuals may have been 'in the labour force' by virtue of the fact that they may have been *seeking* and/or been *available* for work but could not find any. Thirdly, it may be argued that in analysing issues relating to labour supply and demand one cannot assume the actual wage rate to be an exogenous variable, since it is itself determined by market demand and supply forces. If we are to use the wage rate as a regressor, therefore, we must replace it by a suitable instrumental variables estimate.

In the context of U.S. labour supply studies these issues have been resolved by estimating the wage rate on the basis of the personal characteristics of the sample workers (see Rosenzweig, 1980, and the references therein). In the context of labour supply by Indian cultivators, Rosenzweig (*ibid.*) stresses the importance of geographical factors, instead of considering the workers' personal characteristics (which he finds have low explanatory power anyway). This is premised on his observation of relative labour immobility across regions in India. He captures these geographical factors in terms of dummy variables indicating the presence or absence of a local factory, or else local small-scale industry, the distance of the household from such facilities, and whether the household resides in a 'farm development district' (i.e. areas under the purview of some special development programmes such as the Integrated Area Development Programme). In our case, such an exercise would not be possible even if we were to assume, *a priori*, the potential importance of geographical factors. For as we mentioned earlier in this chapter, the mandate villages were purposively selected to ensure that they were not located near towns and highways, did not receive any extraordinary resource transfers, and did not participate in any special development programmes. Bardhan (1984a) resolves this problem by computing a village-wide weighted average wage rate. This, however, would be grossly inadequate in general, since it would erase all household-specific variation in a given village in a given year. Further, it would be impractical in a data set such as ours and others which cover only a small number of villages.

A third method of deriving the wage rate estimates is that of Heckman (1979) who treats both the hours of work as well as the wage rate as endogenous variables, and then estimates them simultaneously using only the nonzero observations. We preferred not to use this method since we feel that the market wage rate is not endogenous to household labour supply decisions.

In the light of the above arguments, we therefore adopted the following way out. Observe that when an individual finds off-farm work, this may be in any of a number of labour markets in the rural sector. In our data set, off-farm work (i.e. work off one's own farm) has been classified into several categories, each of which may be considered an individual labour market in its own right. These categories are crop production, animal husbandry, building and other construction, repairs and maintenance, trade, marketing and transport, domestic work, and other work (such as handicrafts etc.). Unfortunately, this fine categorisation of off-farm work is available only uptil 1978-79. For the subsequent years of the sample, off-farm work has been divided into merely farm-related work, nonfarm related nongovernment work, and nonfarm related government work. Even so, we worked out a weighted average wage rate for each household-year based on employment in these individual labour markets. For those households which did not report any wage rate for a particular year, we then substituted instead, the average wage rate of the remaining households in that particular village in that particular year. The series so obtained was regressed on various socioeconomic, demographic and human capital variables (such as the real product price, age of the household head, education of the household head, caste, family size, number of prime age males, number of prime age females, number of elderly dependent males, number of elderly dependent females, gross cropped area, percentage area irrigated, total input expenditure, nonland assets, coefficient of variation of net revenue and village dummies), to derive estimates of the daily wage rate for each household.[10] These estimates were then deflated by the (weighted average) product price to derive the *estimates of the real wage rate* (RWR, corresponding to w/p_m in the theoretical models).

Finally, to construct the *expected real wage rate* (ERWR) we need, additionally, estimates of the probability of finding employment in the labour market (p^e). The probability of finding employment by the individuals in a given household was derived as the ratio of the actual labour supply to the desired labour supply of the individuals in that household, where desired labour supply was computed as the sum of the actual labour supply and involuntary unemployment. For those households which did not find any off-farm work (but were available and/or seeking it), the probability so computed would be zero. This, however, is not a true reflection of their probability of finding employment. Moreover, since the probability of finding employment would differ on account of differences in age, education, caste etc., household specific estimates were obtained by regressing the actual probabilities on the exogenous variables mentioned in the previous paragraph. The product of the estimated real wage rate and the estimated probability of finding employment gave us estimates of the expected real wage rate.

Notes

1   A 'district' is a sub-division of the state for purposes of revenue administration.

2   The agricultural year 1975-76, for instance, may simply be referred to as 1975 for convenience.

3   A 'taluka' is a sub-division of the district for purposes of revenue administration.

4   Detailed lists of the characteristics considered are given in Singh *et.al.* (1985), appendices I and II.

5   For details of the 'common' cropping patterns see Walker and Subba Rao (1982).

6   Note that we cannot take the logarithms of negative numbers.

7   The current period percentage area under different crops could be another useful regressor (since diversification would lessen risk), the previous period's cropping pattern being captured by lagged net revenue. But the small number of observations per household (only nine) and the lack of relevant data prevented us from doing so.

8   For descriptive purposes the authors categorise the various cropping systems into three broad groups based on the use of improved inputs,

particularly inorganic fertilizer. The three groups are 'traditional', 'semi-improved' and 'improved'.

9   Nor did we find it possible to work it out for ourselves.

10   All these instrumental variables were defined as specified above in the course of outlining the principal features of the sample households.

4 Revenue Risk, Employment Risk and their Local Correlation

The Hypothesis

In Asian agriculture the predominant bulk of farms fall in the 'small' and 'medium' categories. Since these farms are too small to fully, gainfully employ all the available family labour over the agricultural year, they are characterised by substantial amounts of excess labour which can be (and often is) supplied in the daily casual labour market. While on the one hand these farmers are subject to production risk relating to self-cultivation, on the other they are subject to the risk of finding employment in the casual labour market. When considering labour allocation decisions by a farm household, therefore, it is pertinent to consider not *only* the production risk it faces on its own farm (Roe and Graham-Tomasi, 1986; Fafchamps, 1989, 1993; Kanwar, 1991, 1995), or else *only* the uncertainty attaching to market or off-farm labour supply (Bardhan, 1979a, 1984a), but *both* kinds of risks simultaneously. Although we had tentatively assumed the two risks to be independently distributed for developing the farm household production model under risk in chapter 2, we now take a closer look at their possible interdependence and its implications. Even though in a given situation production risk and labour market risk may be independent of each other, in general they may be strongly related in the context of the local casual labour market. The reason for this is not difficult to see. If inimical weather damages crops in a certain region, then not only are the farmers in question victims of this production risk, they are also likely to face greater uncertainty in finding wage employment on other farmers' fields. For the bad weather conditions are likely to affect all the farmers in that (small) region. Of course, this relationship may not be statistically very strong if alternative *nonfarm* sources of wage employment are also available to the farmers, for that would permit them to balance the increased uncertainty of finding *farm-related* work.

The strength of the relationship between these two risks has important implications, firstly, for the correct specification of the farm household model under risk. Not allowing for their interdependence when in fact they are significantly related would lead to a substantial specification bias. On the other hand, allowing for their interdependence would substantially complicate the model and involve making assumptions about the joint distribution of the two risks (see Fackler, 1991; and the references cited therein for the problems involved in estimating such joint distributions). By the same token if these risks are independently distributed, and this is an empirical question, that would help to keep the model relatively simple. Secondly, the interdependence of these risks may also have important implications for the issue of whether the farm household can use the labour market as a hedge against production uncertainty. On the basis of evidence provided by a host of studies relating to various regions of India, Dreze and Mukherjee (1989, p. 246) concluded that '[T]he village labour market is largely closed: labour hiring across neighbouring villages is rare'. They found this to be a pervasive phenomenon in India, including the villages in our sample.[1] Under such circumstances, if the two risks are covariant the possibility of operating in the casual labour market to hedge the production risk that the household faces on its own farm may be relatively small. If, instead, the two risks are independently distributed, the farm household may avail of the opportunities in the local casual labour market to counter the production risk it faces on its own farm. An indirect test of such covariance would be to test for the statistical significance of the farmer's off-farm labour supply response to variations in production risk. If this response is statistically significant it could be interpreted to imply, that although production risk and labour market risk are covariant, their covariance is not strong enough to negate the possibility of using the labour market as a hedge against production uncertainty. Alternatively, if the off-farm labour supply response is found to be statistically *in*significant, this could be taken to indicate that the two risks are significantly covariant. A *direct* test of their interdependence, however, would constitute a more conclusive proof of their covariant relationship, and that is the objective of this chapter.

Our analysis of the data set in the previous chapter showed it to be most appropriate for a study of such issues. The semi-arid environment of the sample households — involving generally poor soils and low and uncertain rainfall — makes for heightened production risks and limited work opportunities. The meagre assets base of the farmers' — both material and human capital — in relation to the number of mouths to feed, as well as their low creditworthiness speak of their limited capacity to mitigate these risks. These characteristics would ensure the existence of both substantial production as well as labour market risks. We commence by considering the definitions of the two risks in the context of the present issue.

Production Risk and Labour Market Risk

We have already defined production risk in terms of crop revenue risk confronting farmers. For farmers, by definition, had crop husbandry as their major occupation and animal husbandry was not an important source of income for them. In chapter 3 we approximated crop revenue risk by the (conditional) coefficient of variation of net revenue (CVNR) estimated for each of the farm households.

The risk associated with labour market employment is captured in terms of the expected real wage rate (ERWR) in the casual labour market, i.e. the product of the probability of finding employment in the local casual labour market and the real wage rate in that market. Labour market uncertainty has been measured thus rather than in terms of the moments of the wage distribution, because the type of risk that is sought to be captured is not the variance of wages around the mean wage for instance, but the less than perfect probability of finding employment in the local casual labour market. In a situation of persistent unemployment and precarious living we feel that it is the uncertainty of finding employment that is comparatively important, rather than the fact that expected wages are low and/or that the wages fluctuate over time. We have already gone over the measurement details of both risk variables in the previous chapter and do not need to repeat them here.

Testing for Stationarity

We propose to test for the dependence of labour market risk on production risk in the 'Granger sense' (Granger, 1981; Engle and Granger, 1987). This exercise consists of two steps. In the first step we determine whether the individual series on production risk and labour market risk are non-stationary. In the second step, using stationary series for both these variables, which may be transforms of the original series in case those were non-stationary, we test for whether production risk 'causes' labour market risk in the Granger sense.

To execute the first step mentioned above, we conduct Dickey-Fuller unit root tests to determine whether the individual series are non-stationary (Dickey and Fuller, 1979, 1981). For a series Y_t this essentially amounts to testing whether the coefficient of Y_{t-1} in a regression of ΔY_t on Y_{t-1} equals zero, such a regression being called the 'Dickey-Fuller regression'. Since the distribution of the test statistic in this case is found to be affected by the presence or absence of a constant term unless a trend variable is also present in the equation, it is often preferred to include both a constant and a trend term in the regression. Phillips (1987) shows that the validity of these tests depends crucially on the error process not being autocorrelated, although heteroscedasticity is not a problem. In case the errors are autocorrelated, lagged terms of the dependent variable are added incrementally to the set of regressors till serial independence is achieved. This entails estimating the so-called 'Augmented Dickey-Fuller regression' equation:

$$\Delta Y_t = \alpha_0 + \alpha_1 t + \alpha_2 Y_{t-1} + \Sigma_k \, \delta_k \Delta Y_{t-k} + \epsilon_t \qquad (4.1)$$

where regressor t is the time trend, k denotes the number of lags and the error term $\epsilon_t \sim NIID(0, \, \sigma_\epsilon^2)$. Since we had panel data, we pooled the cross-section and time series observations by using a variation of the 'dummy variables or fixed effects model', i.e. by using a separate intercept term for each of the three villages. The economic rationale for preferring this mode of pooling the observations is discussed at greater length in chapters 5 and 6, where its relevance is heightened in the context of labour demand and supply decisions by the rural households.[2] It is only for the sake of convenience that we have written the intercept as a single constant term.

Using the errors from the Dickey-Fuller regressions for each of the two series, we tested for serial correlation using the Durbin 'large sample test'.[3] In the case of both variables, ERWR as well as CVNR, the error term was found to be serially independent,[4] obviating the need to run augmented Dickey-Fuller regressions. We then used the Dickey-Fuller regression results for CVNR and ERWR to conduct the stationarity tests, and the results are presented in Table 4.1. The results show that the two series are stationary. Consider the results for the expected real wage rate. The null hypothesis of a unit root can be rejected only if the computed test statistic is smaller than the critical value. The test statistic for the null hypothesis $\alpha_2 = 0$ equals -11.97 which is much smaller than the 10% critical value $t = -3.13$. Further, the test statistics for the hypotheses $\alpha_0 = \alpha_1 = \alpha_2 = 0$

Table 4.1 Dickey-Fuller tests for stationarity — all households

Variable: Expected real wage rate (ERWR)
Number of lagged dependent terms = 0; Number of observations = 424

Null hypothesis	Test statistic	Asymptotic 10% critical value
$\alpha_2 = 0$	-11.97	-3.13
$\alpha_0 = \alpha_1 = \alpha_2 = 0$	34.92	4.03
$\alpha_1 = \alpha_2 = 0$	78.64	5.34

Variable: Coefficient of variation of net revenue (CVNR)
Number of lagged dependent terms = 0; Number of observations = 424

Null hypothesis	Test statistic	Asymptotic 10% critical value
$\alpha_2 = 0$	20.92	-3.13
$\alpha_0 = \alpha_1 = \alpha_2 = 0$	87.71	4.03
$\alpha_1 = \alpha_2 = 0$	219.21	5.34

(unit root without drift) and $\alpha_1 = \alpha_2 = 0$ (unit root with drift) are 34.92 and 78.64, which are significant at the 10% level since they exceed the respective critical values $F = 4.03$ and $F = 5.34$. Similar observations may be made for the variable CVNR. Thus, we reject the null hypothesis of a unit root in the case of both the variables in question. In other words, their time series may be taken to be stationary.

Testing for Granger Causality — Aggregate Data

Let the unrestricted causal model relating the two variables ERWR and CVNR be represented as:

$$\text{ERWR}_t = \alpha_0 + \alpha_1 t + \Sigma_{i=1}^{I} \beta_i \text{ERWR}_{t-i} + \Sigma_{j=0}^{J} \gamma_j \text{CVNR}_{t-j} + u_t \quad (4.2a)$$

$$\text{CVNR}_t = \alpha_0' + \alpha_1' t + \Sigma_{k=1}^{K} \beta_k \text{CVNR}_{t-k} + \Sigma_{l=0}^{L} \gamma_l \text{ERWR}_{t-l} + v_t \quad (4.2b)$$

where u_t and v_t are independently distributed Gaussian processes. In testing whether variable CVNR 'causes' variable ERWR we also need to

Table 4.2 Final prediction errors — all households

ERWR: Expected real wage rate

j↓\ i→	0	1	2	3
–	0.3182244	0.2852775	0.2869917	0.2696092
0	0.3182049	0.2852635	0.2869742	0.2695919
1	0.3196487	0.2865778	0.2882966	0.2701665
2	0.3188255	0.2843972	0.2861190	0.2684080
3	0.3203250	0.2861719	0.2878969	0.2701019

CVNR: Coefficient of variation of net revenue

l↓\ k→	0	1	2	3
–	456.2817	459.0720	461.9215	464.8315
0	456.2537	459.0394	461.8955	464.8062
1	459.1317	461.9352	464.8082	467.7380
2	461.0146	463.8299	466.7095	469.6538
3	463.9221	466.7524	469.6504	472.6138

test that the reverse causation does not obtain. Some researchers argue that such bivariate causality tests are inadequate and that other relevant explanatory variables should also be included in the equations of the above model (Darrat, 1988; Lutkepohl, 1992). This criticism, we feel, need not hold in the case of all causal relationships. For instance, in our specific case, it is not immediately obvious what other variables should be included in explaining production risk, i.e. the dependent variable in equation (4.2b). To appreciate this difficulty consider a stripped-down definition of production risk in terms of rainfall variability alone. Surely, none of the farm household variables such as the farmer's age, education, assets etc. can be taken to affect rainfall variability. On the other hand, one can indeed argue that there are variables other than production risk that may 'explain' labour market risk, i.e. the dependent variable in equation (4.2a). But considering our short time series of only nine years, we are unable to include even some of these other explanatory variables in our causality framework, each of which may appear with several lags.

To estimate model (4.2a)-(4.2b) we need to determine the appropriate lag order for the variables in each equation. This we do by using the Akaike Final Prediction Error criterion (Hsiao, 1979; Judge *et.al.*, 1988).[5]

Taking a maximum lag length of three periods,[6] we estimate the Final Prediction Errors for both our variables and the results are given in Table 4.2. The first rows of both panels in the table give the final prediction errors for the dependent variable regressed on itself, lagged various periods.[7] The subsequent rows give the final prediction errors for the dependent variable regressed on itself *as well as* on the hypothesized causal variable, lagged various periods.[8] For variable ERWR the lag combination (3, 2) has the minimum final prediction error, while for variable CVNR the optimum lag combination is (0, 0). Therefore, the appropriate estimation equations for these two variables may be specified as:

$$ERWR_t = \alpha_0 + \alpha_1 t + \beta_1 ERWR_{t-1} + \beta_2 ERWR_{t-2} + \beta_3 ERWR_{t-3}$$

$$+ \gamma_0 CVNR_t + \gamma_1 CVNR_{t-1} + \gamma_2 CVNR_{t-2} + u_t \qquad (4.3a)$$

$$CVNR_t = \alpha_0' + \alpha_1' t + \gamma_0' ERWR_t + v_t \qquad (4.3b)$$

At this juncture we would like to point out that the manner in which the final prediction error criterion is used in the literature may not be entirely satisfactory. We feel that when we hypothesize some variable y_t to be Granger caused by some other variable x_t and are desirous of testing for this causality, then x_t should be included as a regressor anyway. In other words, the inclusion of x_t follows directly from the hypothesis being tested; which, in turn, is presumably grounded in economic intuition. To put it more strongly, even if the Akaike information criterion tells us not to include x_t (because $FPE[y_{t-1}] < FPE[y_{t-1}, x_t]$, i.e. the final prediction error including the supposedly causal variable x_t exceeds the final prediction error otherwise), x_t should be included because the null hypothesis requires its inclusion. Unless, of course, the null hypothesis itself rules this out by stating that the causality relationship between y_t and x_t is not contemporaneous. Having included x_t in the estimation equation, only the inclusion of further (lagged) terms should be based on some 'objective' criterion such as Akaike's, because economic intuition may not have anything to add to their case.

Having determined the specific model for estimation, we now test for Granger causality. Of the various causality tests suggested in the literature, the Granger test (Granger, 1969; Sargent, 1976) appears to be a relatively preferred choice. This is partly supported by the available Monte Carlo evidence which reveals the Granger test to be more powerful than the Sims

Table 4.3 Granger causality tests — all households

Panel A: Single equation estimation
Dependent variable: ERWR — LMF statistic = 1.765
Dependent variable: CVNR — LMF statistic = 0.019

Panel B: SUR estimation
Dependent variable: Expected real rage rate (ERWR)

Variable*	Estimated coefficient	Standard error	P-value
T	0.197	0.023	0.000
$ERWR_{t-1}$	0.298	0.063	0.000
$ERWR_{t-2}$	−0.090	0.069	0.197
$ERWR_{t-3}$	0.487	0.102	0.000
$CVNR_t$	0.0004	0.001	0.795
$CVNR_{t-1}$	0.002	0.001	0.266
$CVNR_{t-2}$	−0.003	0.001	0.046

R^2 = 0.5481; σ = 0.5166; ln(L) = −1659.84
H_0: CVNR does not granger cause ERWR — F statistic = 1.796; P-value = 0.147

Dependent variable: Coefficient of variation of net revenue (CVNR)

Variable*	Estimated coefficient	Standard error	P-value
T	0.377	0.863	0.662
$ERWR_t$	0.539	2.149	0.802

R^2 = 0.0113; σ = 21.463; ln(L) = −1659.840
H_0: ERWR does not granger cause CVNR — F statistic = 0.063; P-value = 0.802
* Regression estimates for constant terms are not reported; a separate intercept was used for each of the villages.

test and tests based on cross-correlation procedures (Guilkey and Salemi, 1982; Nelson and Schwert, 1982). Furthermore, the Granger test is relatively parsimonious in its data requirements — the Sims test resulting in fewer degrees of freedom both on account of observations lost in estimation (since the most recent observations are retained for constructing the 'leading variables'), as well as on account of the larger number of parameters to be estimated (namely, for the leading variables).

To conduct the Granger test we proceed as follows. Consider equation (4.3a) in the above model. We first regress $ERWR_t$ on the time trend, $ERWR_{t-1}$, $ERWR_{t-2}$ and $ERWR_{t-3}$. The residuals obtained from this regression are then regressed on all the regressors, i.e. on the time trend, $ERWR_{t-1}$, $ERWR_{t-2}$, $ERWR_{t-3}$ as well as $CVNR_t$, $CVNR_{t-1}$ and $CVNR_{t-2}$. Computing the coefficient of determination from this regression, we construct the *LMF* statistic or the Lagrange Multiplier statistic in its *F*-distribution form, as $LMF = ((T-h)/k)(R^2/(1-R^2))$, where T is the actual number of observations used in the estimation (318 for model 4.3a–4.3b, which is less than the total number of observations available because of the presence of lagged variables), h is the total number of parameters estimated, and k is the number of terms of the supposedly causal variable (Charemza and Deadman, 1993). Under the null hypothesis, this statistic is distributed as F(k, T–h). From Table 4.3, panel A we find that *LMF* = 1.765 for variable ERWR, which is smaller than the 5% critical value $F(3, 308) = 2.621$. In other words, we cannot reject the null hypothesis of the joint insignificance of $CVNR_t$, $CVNR_{t-1}$ and $CVNR_{t-2}$ in Granger causing $ERWR_t$. Similarly, we note that $LMF = 0.019$ for variable CVNR, which falls short of the 5% critical value $F(1, 313) = 3.777$. This implies that we cannot reject the null hypothesis of the insignificance of $ERWR_t$ in Granger causing $CVNR_t$.

An alternative method of conducting the Granger test is to estimate model 4.3a–4.3b as a system, by the seemingly unrelated regression (SUR) method, and then use the *F*-test for exclusion restrictions to test for the insignificance of one or the other explanatory variables. The system estimation results are presented in panel B of Table 4.3. Again we cannot reject the null hypothesis of the joint insignificance of $CVNR_t$, $CVNR_{t-1}$ and $CVNR_{t-2}$ in granger causing $ERWR_t$, because the associated test statistic $F = 1.796$ has a *p*-value of 0.147. Similarly, the reverse causality in not found to hold, the associated *F*-statistic (= 0.063) having a *p*-value of 0.802. The problem with this procedure is, however, that in dynamic models the error terms cannot really be taken to be independent of the lagged dependent variables, so that the *F*-statistic is no longer distributed according to its nominal distribution (see Davidson and Mackinnon, 1993). Furthermore, as we pointed out above, in our specific case the reverse causality of labour market risk affecting production risk does not appear to

Table 4.4   Final prediction errors — individual villages

Aurepalle

ERWR: Expected real wage rate

$j\downarrow\setminus i\rightarrow$	0	1	2	3
–	0.0820769	0.0644400	0.0627211	0.0601118
0	0.0813202	0.0638068	0.0623161	0.0598723
1	0.0817518	0.0641344	0.0626277	0.0601481
2	0.0822512	0.0644268	0.0629088	0.0602481
3	0.0825528	0.0646659	0.0631062	0.0605154

CVNR: Coefficient of variation of net revenue

$l\downarrow\setminus k\rightarrow$	0	1	2	3
–	3.794174	3.726006	3.576546	3.598239
0	3.759194	3.695780	3.546941	3.567863
1	3.779360	3.716130	3.563312	3.584263
2	3.766652	3.702909	3.553532	3.574894
3	3.771086	3.705433	3.567954	3.589067

Shirapur

ERWR: Expected real wage rate

$j\downarrow\setminus i\rightarrow$	0	1	2	3
–	0.1255342	0.1212250	0.1210370	0.1111378
0	0.1254956	0.1212016	0.1209761	0.1110847
1	0.1259158	0.1216052	0.1213816	0.1106432
2	0.1239763	0.1189490	0.1186452	0.1086967
3	0.1243189	0.1195990	0.1193620	0.1093497

CVNR: Coefficient of variation of net revenue

$l\downarrow\setminus k\rightarrow$	0	1	2	3
–	449.3927	452.0804	454.8844	457.7527
0	449.2546	451.9562	454.7323	457.6012
1	451.9664	454.6828	457.4959	460.3823
2	450.5855	453.2954	456.0667	458.8785
3	453.4277	456.1550	458.9436	461.7747

Table 4.4 continued

Kanzara

ERWR: Expected real wage rate

j↓\ i→	0	1	2	3
–	0.1004659	0.0906150	0.0911746	0.0857439
0	0.1001938	0.0906004	0.0911576	0.0857438
1	0.1008057	0.0911687	0.0917291	0.0860372
2	0.1008725	0.0912884	0.0918518	0.0863261
3	0.1014268	0.0918643	0.0924314	0.0868476

CVNR: Coefficient of variation of net revenue

l↓\ k→	0	1	2	3
–	0.0841174	0.0724880	0.0727632	0.0710472
0	0.0838895	0.0723550	0.0726517	0.0709667
1	0.0833203	0.0721245	0.0724230	0.0709517
2	0.0833087	0.0722718	0.0725656	0.0711946
3	0.0836464	0.0725999	0.0728791	0.0714391

make economic sense. Consequently, we would not like the parameter estimates of equation (4.3a) to be constrained by the parameter estimates of equation (4.3b); that is, we would not like to estimate equations (4.3a) and (4.3b) simultaneously, although this may make more sense in the case of other relationships. For both the above reasons, we prefer to use the *LMF* statistic outlined earlier in testing for Granger causality, and therefore consider it more appropriate to base our conclusions on it. Putting together these results, we conclude that the variables ERWR and CVNR are causally *un*related in the Granger sense. More specifically, we do not find any evidence of the dependence of labour market risk (ERWR) on production risk (CVNR).

Testing for Granger Causality – Disaggregated Village-level Data

We know from chapter 3 that our sample comprises households from three different villages with diverse agroclimatic characteristics. Therefore, the natural question to ask would be whether the causality relationship that we found above for the aggregate data (or rather the lack of it), would also hold for the disaggregated village-level data. It is this question to which we turn in this section. As before, the first step involves the determination of the optimum lag order for each of the two variables ERWR and CVNR, for each of the three villages of Aurepalle, Shirapur and Kanzara. From the final prediction errors reported in Table 4.4, we find that for Aurepalle the optimum lag combination is (3, 0) for variable ERWR, and (2, 0) for variable CVNR. The estimation model (with 108 observations available for actual use) is:

$$ERWR_t = \alpha_0 + \alpha_1 t + \beta_1 ERWR_{t-1} + \beta_2 ERWR_{t-2} + \beta_3 ERWR_{t-3}$$

$$+ \gamma_0 CVNR_t + u_t \tag{4.4a}$$

$$CVNR_t = \alpha_0' + \alpha_1' t + \beta_1' CVNR_{t-1} + \beta_2' CVNR_{t-2} + \gamma_0' ERWR_t$$
$$+ v_t \tag{4.4b}$$

In the case of Shirapur, the optimum lag combinations for variables ERWR and CVNR turn out to be, respectively, (3, 2) and (0, 0). This yields the following estimating equations (leaving us with 78 observations for use in estimation):

$$ERWR_t = \alpha_0 + \alpha_1 t + \beta_1 ERWR_{t-1} + \beta_2 ERWR_{t-2} + \beta_3 ERWR_{t-3}$$

$$+ \gamma_0 CVNR_t + \gamma_1 CVNR_{t-1} + \gamma_2 CVNR_{t-2} + u_t \tag{4.5a}$$

$$CVNR_t = \alpha_0' + \alpha_1' t + \gamma_0' ERWR_t + v_t \tag{4.5b}$$

And for village Kanzara, the optimum lag combinations are (3, 0) and (3, 1) for ERWR and CVNR, respectively. The estimation equations are:

$$ERWR_t = \alpha_0 + \alpha_1 t + \beta_1 ERWR_{t-1} + \beta_2 ERWR_{t-2} + \beta_3 ERWR_{t-3}$$

$$+ \gamma_0 CVNR_t + u_t \tag{4.6a}$$

$$CVNR_t = \alpha_0' + \alpha_1' t + \beta_1' CVNR_{t-1} + \beta_2' CVNR_{t-2} + \beta_3' CVNR_{t-3}$$

$$+ \gamma_0' ERWR_t + \gamma_1' ERWR_{t-1} + v_t \tag{4.6b}$$

(with 132 observations available for estimation). We have used the same

Table 4.5 Granger causality tests — village Aurepalle

Panel A: Single equation estimation
Dependent variable: ERWR — LMF statistic = 0.408
Dependent variable: CVNR — LMF statistic = 0.860

Panel B: SUR estimation
Dependent variable: Expected real wage rate (ERWR)

Variable	Estimated coefficient	Standard error	P-value
Constant	-12.323	2.543	0.000
T	0.154	0.031	0.000
$ERWR_{t-1}$	0.404	0.124	0.002
$ERWR_{t-2}$	0.128	0.137	0.355
$ERWR_{t-3}$	0.298	0.137	0.032
$CVNR_t$	0.016	0.012	0.193

$R^2 = 0.4831$; $\sigma = 0.4276$; $\ln(L) = -335.683$
H_0: CVNR does not granger cause ERWR — F statistic = 1.716; P-value = 0.192.

Dependent variable: Coefficient of variation of net revenue (CVNR)

Variable	Estimated coefficient	Standard error	P-value
Constant	12.231	17.670	0.490
T	-0.153	0.219	0.487
$CVNR_{t-1}$	0.118	0.091	0.199
$CVNR_{t-2}$	0.194	0.089	0.032
$ERWR_t$	0.978	0.645	0.132

$R^2 = 0.0738$; $\sigma = 3.2837$; $\ln(L) = -335.683$
H_0: ERWR does not granger cause CVNR — F statistic = 2.300; P-value = 0.131.

symbols for the equation parameters for all three villages for the sake of convenience.

Using the models specified above — namely (4.4a)-(4.4b) for village

Table 4.6 Granger causality tests — village Shirapur

Panel A: Single equation estimation
Dependent variable: ERWR — LMF statistic = 2.478
Dependent variable: CVNR — LMF statistic = 0.023

Panel B: SUR estimation
Dependent variable: Expected real wage rate (ERWR)

Variable	Estimated coefficient	Standard error	P-value
Constant	-26.429	5.132	0.000
T	0.335	0.064	0.000
$ERWR_{t-1}$	0.196	0.126	0.125
$ERWR_{t-2}$	-0.231	0.142	0.108
$ERWR_{t-3}$	0.633	0.237	0.009
$CVNR_t$	-0.001	0.002	0.748
$CVNR_{t-1}$	0.002	0.002	0.402
$CVNR_{t-2}$	-0.002	0.002	0.189

$R^2 = 0.4833$; $\sigma = 0.6897$; $\ln(L) = -480.839$
H_o: CVNR does not granger cause ERWR — F statistic = 0.878; P-value = 0.454

Dependent variable: Coefficient of variation of net revenue (CVNR)

Variable	Estimated coefficient	Standard error	P-value
Constant	-239.010	298.800	0.426
T	2.912	3.739	0.439
$ERWR_t$	-1.929	7.025	0.784

$R^2 = 0.0083$; $\sigma = 43.512$; $\ln(L) = -480.839$
H_o: ERWR does not granger cause CVNR — F statistic = 0.075; P-value = 0.784

Aurepalle, (4.5a)-(4.5b) for Shirapur and (4.6a)-(4.6b) for Kanzara — we now conduct Granger causality tests for each of the three villages. The LMF statistics are presented in panel A of Tables 4.5, 4.6 and 4.7. In the

Table 4.7 Granger causality tests — village Kanzara

Panel A: Single equation estimation
Dependent variable: ERWR — LMF statistic = 0.0001
Dependent variable: CVNR — LMF statistic = 0.958

Panel B: SUR estimation
Dependent variable: Expected real wage rate (ERWR)

Variable	Estimated coefficient	Standard error	P-value
Constant	-12.866	2.857	0.000
T	0.164	0.035	0.000
$ERWR_{t-1}$	0.291	0.096	0.003
$ERWR_{t-2}$	-0.107	0.101	0.289
$ERWR_{t-3}$	0.553	0.186	0.004
$CVNR_t$	-0.011	0.090	0.903

R^2 = 0.4575; σ = 0.4594; ln(L) = -150.116
H_o: CVNR does not granger cause ERWR — F statistic = 0.015; P-value = 0.903

Dependent variable: Coefficient of variation of net revenue (CVNR)

Variable	Estimated coefficient	Standard error	P-value
Constant	0.374	2.506	0.001
T	-0.099	0.031	0.002
$CVNR_{t-1}$	0.269	0.073	0.000
$CVNR_{t-2}$	0.002	0.046	0.965
$CVNR_{t-3}$	0.026	0.014	0.067
$ERWR_t$	-0.005	0.078	0.944
$ERWR_{t-1}$	0.081	0.085	0.344

R^2 = 0.3288; σ = 0.4183; log(L) = -150.116
H_o: ERWR does not granger cause CVNR — F statistic = 0.481; P-value = 0.619

case of village Aurepalle (Table 4.5, panel A), the LMF statistic for variable ERWR is estimated to be 0.408 which is much smaller than the 5% critical value $F(1, 102) = 3.840$. For variable CVNR, $LMF = 0.86$ which is smaller than the 5% critical value $F(1, 103) = 3.839$. Thus, we do not find any evidence of CVNR granger causing ERWR. Similarly, for Shirapur (Table 4.6, panel A) the LMF statistics for ERWR and CVNR are, respectively, 2.478 and 0.023, which are both less than their corresponding 5% critical values. And for Kanzara (Table 4.7, panel A), the LMF statistics for variables ERWR and CVNR are 0.0001 and 0.958, both being insignificant at the 5% level. These conclusions are strongly supported by the F-test results from the alternative SUR estimation procedure reported in panel B of Tables 4.5, 4.6 and 4.7. Therefore, even for the disaggregated village-level data we do *not* find any evidence of labour market risk depending on production risk.

Testing for Granger Causality — Disaggregation by Gender

Finally we consider the covariance of labour market risk with production risk for female and male labour separately. Female labour constitutes a substantial proportion of the labour sold by cultivator households in our study villages, averaging about 76% of the total labour days sold over the period 1975-76/1984-85 (considering only those cultivator households which reported positive labour market participation). From the final prediction errors reported in Table 4.8 we find the optimum lag combination to be (3, 2) for variable ERWR and (3, 0) for variable CVNR, both in the case of female as well as male labour. Therefore, the estimation model for both female and male labour is:

$$ERWR_t = \alpha_0 + \alpha_1 t + \beta_1 ERWR_{t-1} + \beta_2 ERWR_{t-2} + \beta_3 ERWR_{t-3}$$

$$+ \gamma_0 CVNR_t + \gamma_1 CVNR_{t-1} + \gamma_2 CVNR_{t-2} + u_t \qquad (4.7a)$$

$$CVNR_t = \alpha_0' + \alpha_1' t + \gamma_0' ERWR_t + v_t \qquad (4.7b)$$

(leaving us with 318 observations for estimation). In the case of female labour (Table 4.9), the LMF statistic for ERWR is 2.264 which is smaller than the 5% critical value of $F(3, 308) = 2.621$; and $LMF = 0.002$ for CVNR, which is much smaller than the 5% critical value $F(1, 313) = 3.777$. Thus, there is no evidence of CVNR granger causing ERWR. For male labour (Table 4.10), LMF is 2.3020 for variable ERWR

Table 4.8 Final prediction errors — females and males

Females

ERWR: Expected real wage rate

j↓\ i→	0	1	2	3
–	0.10340430	0.06794170	0.06706739	0.06455352
0	0.10340350	0.06794124	0.06706550	0.06455271
1	0.10402300	0.06833738	0.06745393	0.06490087
2	0.10359360	0.06730931	0.06645220	0.06396031
3	0.10420590	0.06759331	0.06680566	0.06430295

CVNR

l↓\ k→	0	1	2	3
–	456.2817	459.0720	461.9215	464.8315
0	456.2783	459.0692	461.9158	464.8256
1	459.1269	461.9340	464.8063	467.7320
2	461.8421	464.6639	467.5544	470.5033
3	463.9425	466.7973	469.6979	472.6607

Males

ERWR: Expected real wage rate

j↓\ i→	0	1	2	3
–	0.3634808	0.2844833	0.2816436	0.2513037
0	0.3634298	0.2844516	0.2816432	0.2512914
1	0.3656461	0.2861265	0.2833035	0.2519732
2	0.3635154	0.2825261	0.2798756	0.2489037
3	0.3657991	0.2833146	0.2809699	0.2496431

CVNR: Coefficient of variation of net revenue

l↓\ k→	9	1	2	3
–	456.2817	459.0720	461.9215	464.8315
0	456.2176	459.0097	461.8454	464.7552
1	459.0960	461.9058	464.7591	467.6878
2	459.5172	462.3302	465.1824	468.1142
3	462.1497	464.9368	467.8123	470.7631

Table 4.9 Granger causality tests — females

Panel A: Single equation estimation
Dependent variable: ERWR — LMF statistic = 2.264
Dependent variable: CVNR — LMF statistic = 0.002

Panel B: SUR estimation
Dependent variable: Expected real wage rate (ERWR)

Variable[*]	Estimated coefficient	Standard error	P-value
T	0.066	0.010	0.000
$ERWR_{t-1}$	0.508	0.064	0.000
$ERWR_{t-2}$	0.069	0.075	0.353
$ERWR_{t-3}$	0.308	0.082	0.000
$CVNR_t$	-0.0001	0.001	0.907
$CVNR_{t-1}$	0.0003	0.001	0.615
$CVNR_{t-2}$	-0.002	0.001	0.011

$R^2 = 0.5368$; $\sigma = 0.2522$; $\ln(L) = -1431.84$
H_0: CVNR does not granger cause ERWR — F statistic = 2.284; P-value = 0.078

Dependent variable: Coefficient of variation of net revenue (CVNR)

Variable[*]	Estimated coefficient	Standard error	P-value
T	0.530	0.801	0.509
$ERWR_t$	-0.287	3.770	0.939

$R^2 = 0.0113$; $\sigma = 21.463$; $\ln(L) = -1431.84$
H_0: ERWR does not granger cause CVNR — F statistic = 0.006; P-value = 0.939
[*] Regression estimates for constant terms not reported because a separate intercept was used for each of the villages.

and 0.044 for variable CVNR (the critical values being the same as in the case of female labour). Again, these results are supported by the *F*-statistics computed from the alternative SUR estimation procedure. Therefore, in the

Table 4.10 Granger causality tests — males

Panel A: Single equation estimation
Dependent variable: ERWR — LMF statistic = 2.302
Dependent variable: CVNR — LMF statistic = 0.044

Panel B: SUR estimation
Dependent variable: Expected real wage rate (ERWR)

Variable*	Estimated coefficient	Standard error	P-value
T	0.180	0.020	0.000
$ERWR_{t-1}$	0.308	0.058	0.000
$ERWR_{t-2}$	-0.015	0.063	0.808
$ERWR_{t-3}$	0.532	0.083	0.000
$CVNR_t$	-0.0001	0.001	0.954
$CVNR_{t-1}$	0.001	0.001	0.304
$CVNR_{t-2}$	-0.003	0.001	·0.017

R^2 = 0.6329; σ = 0.4975; ln(L) = −1647.80
H_o: CVNR does not granger cause ERWR — F statistic = 2.316; P-value = 0.075

Dependent variable: Coefficient of variation of net revenue (CVNR)

Variable*	Estimated coefficient	Standard error	P-value
T	0.646	0.821	0.432
$ERWR_t$	-0.698	2.010	0.729

R^2 = 0.0113 σ = 21.462; ln(L) = −1647.80
H_o: ERWR does not granger cause CVNR — F statistic = 0.121; P-value = 0.728

* Regression estimates for constant terms not reported because a separate intercept was used for each of the villages.

case of both female and male casual labour we do not find evidence of production risk granger causing labour market risk. This supports our earlier findings using aggregate as well as disaggregated village-level data.

Gathering these results together, we conclude that variations in production risk do not statistically significantly explain variations in labour market risk for our sample of cultivator households.

Some Tentative Explanations

This is hardly a self-evident result. Considering the cultivators' meagre assets base (primarily land) and large family size, we would expect them to be significant contributors of labour to the casual labour market, such that wage labour earnings constitute an important proportion of their total incomes. And indeed, using another ICRISAT sample (of which ours is a subset), Walker and Ryan (1990, p. 70) report that '... cultivator households ... relied heavily on labour market earnings primarily in the village labour market for casual *agricultural* labour' (emphasis added). This implies that if cultivation were to be negatively affected by production risk this, in turn, would negatively affect the demand for casual agricultural labour and hence cause a reduction in the probability of finding employment. In other words, normally we would expect production risk to translate into labour market risk, in the context of largely closed village labour markets as in our sample regions.

Even when production risk and labour market risk are covariant, however, this link may not be sufficiently strong if production risk is small. And production risk may be small either when rainfall is assured and/or because the village in question is relatively irrigated, and has good, fertile soils. From our discussion in chapter 3 recall that only village Kanzara had relatively high and assured rainfall, whereas both villages Aurepalle and Shirapur had rather scanty and erratic rainfall. Only in two years out of 10 was total annual rainfall less than 700mm in Kanzara, whereas in Aurepalle and Shirapur this was true in seven and six years out of 10, respectively. Whereas the mean annual rainfall was only a little over 600mm in both Aurepalle and Shirapur, in Kanzara it averaged close to 900mm over the 10 year sample period. Whereas Kanzara had deep black soils (with high moisture-retention capacity), Shirapur had medium to deep black soils, and Aurepalle had red soils (with poor moisture-retention capacity). Moreover, these villages were not irrigated to any significant extent. Whereas about 13% of Kanzara's cultivated area was irrigated, in Aurepalle and Shirapur this proportion averaged only around 9%. Thus, although yield risk may have been relatively less in Kanzara as compared to Aurepalle and Shirapur, production risks are quite unlikely to have been small in either of the three villages. Therefore, one would expect *a priori*, that the high yield risk in these villages (at least in Aurepalle and Shirapur) would translate into a high labour market risk. Our empirical exercises, however, relate a different story. Since we don't find this relationship to be statistically significant, in an effort to reconcile the empirical findings with our commonsense expectations we must ask what factors may have weakened it.

First, the labour market may offer not just agriculture-related work but nonfarm work as well. For the sake of argument, consider the situation where the labour market offers farm-related work only. Under these circumstances, if production prospects were to be depressed by poor rainfall, this would translate into an increased lack of work in the labour market (since the only kind of work available is farm-related work). Therefore, we would expect production risk to affect labour market risk just as we argued above. Now suppose, more realistically, that both farm-related work as well as nonfarm work are available in the casual labour market. In this case, although production risk may negatively affect the availability of farm-related work, it may not affect the availability of nonfarm work, at least not to the same extent. Consequently, the relation between production risk and labour market risk would be weakened. Of course, what is more relevant is the *income* from nonfarm work as a proportion of total off-farm income, rather than the availability of nonfarm work *per se*.

In addition to the casual *agricultural* labour market, our sample of owner-cultivators also worked in activities such as animal husbandry, marketing, transport and services, repairs and maintenance, building and construction, and other work (such as handicrafts etc.). For the three villages taken together,[9] although an overwhelming 78% of off-farm (i.e. off-own-farm) casual labour days were devoted to agriculture-related work, a fairly substantial 22% were accounted for by non-agricultural activities. At the village level, the picture was fairly heterogenous. While in Shirapur non-agricultural activities accounted for as much as 62% of the total casual labour days supplied, in Kanzara and Aurepalle this proportion amounted to only 12% and 4%, respectively. The relative contributions of farm-related and nonfarm work in total wages accruing from off-farm employment closely reflected the employment figures. For all three villages together, nonfarm activities accounted for 23% of the wages earned from off-farm casual labour. In Shirapur this figure was as high as 63%, whereas in Kanzara and Aurepalle it was a more modest 13% and 6%, respectively. Thus, atleast in Kanzara and Shirapur nonfarm activities contributed a 'reasonably large' share of the total employment and wages from off-farm casual labour.

Second, note that in our empirical exercises production risk has not been captured merely in terms of rainfall or yield variability, as it usually is in studies relating to agriculture. Instead, net revenue variability is considered to be the more appropriate production risk measure. Recall from chapter 3 that this is partly because of the fact that all households in a specific village normally experience the same rainfall, whereas what we wanted was a household-specific risk measure. Moreover, since households differ in their capacity to combat given objective risks, the subjective household production risk corresponding to a given objective risk (such as rainfall variability) would vary between households. But more importantly, production risk arises not only due to rainfall or even yield variability, but price variability as well. It was found that in most of the unirrigated semi-arid tropical districts, yield and price are negatively covariant (Walker and Ryan, 1990, p. 228), so that yield variability *may possibly* exceed net revenue variability. In such a case, production risk would be relatively smaller if it is measured in terms of net revenue variability (as we have done), than if it were measured in terms of yield variability or rainfall variability alone. Unfortunately, we were unable to test this proposition empirically, because yield data were unavailable to us. Quite possibly, both the above reasons may have been behind our finding of a statistically insignificant relation between production risk and labour market risk for our sample cultivators.

Of course, one could further test the hypothesis that production risk is related to the risk of finding cultivation-related work *per se* in the casual labour market. But we were prevented from doing so by the unavailability of data to compute the 'probability of finding cultivation-related employment' as distinct from the 'probability of finding employment'[10] in the casual labour market. In any case, this would still leave the larger issue of the dependence of labour market risk on production risk unaddressed. Our empirical finding has at least two important implications. Theoretically, in modelling labour allocation decisions by the farm household we need not consider the joint distribution of production and labour market risks. Assuming them to be independently distributed makes the model easier to specify and estimate, as in chapter 2 above, because no assumptions need be made about their joint distribution. Empirically, given the insulated nature of village labour markets (in India), it raises the possibility of the farm household hedging against production risk through variations in its wage labour effort.

Notes

1   Why the rural labour markets in India are so insulated is an interesting, but separate, question.

2   In any case, using a separate intercept term for each of the households does not alter our conclusions (see Kanwar, 1994).

3   This involved regressing the residuals obtained from the Dickey-Fuller regression equations (ϵ_t) on the residuals lagged one period (ϵ_{t-1}), and the other regressors (namely t and Y_{t-1}). The significance of the lagged residuals term is then determined in the usual manner.

4   The coefficient of ϵ_{t-1} has an associated t-value of -1.346 in the case of variable ERWR and -0.1774 in the case of variable CVNR. Both are insignificant at even the 10% level.

5   Judge *et.al.* (1988) point out that Hsiao's original method may not always be able to identify the optimum lag order. Thus, in practice, it may identify a lag order which is not associated with the minimum final prediction error. A (likelihood ratio) test may then have to be conducted to choose between the lag combination suggested by Hsiao's method and the one corresponding to the minimum FPE. This is the procedure followed by us.

6   We chose the maximum lag to be three periods on account of the rather short time series that we have (just nine periods), although degrees of freedom are not a problem on account of the large cross-section.

7   The Final Prediction Error in this case is computed as:
$$FPE(i) = [(T + i + 1)/(T - i - 1)]\ [RSS/T]$$
where T is the actual number of observations used in estimation, i is the lag length, and RSS is the residual sum of squares. As the lag length increases, the first term in the above expression increases but the second term decreases. These opposing factors are assumed to be balanced optimally when their product, the FPE, reaches a minimum.

8   The Final Prediction Error is now computed as:
$$FPE(i, j) = [(T + i + j + 1)/T - i - j - 1)]\ [RSS/T]$$
where j is the lag length pertaining to the causal variable, and the other variables are as defined earlier.

9   The figures cited in this paragraph refer to the period 1979-84. The break-down of off-farm work into agriculture-related and nonfarm work was not available to us for the earlier years of this sample.

10 Recall that the probability of finding employment was computed as the ratio of the actual labour supply to the desired labour supply, where

desired labour supply was itself measured as the sum of the actual labour supply and involuntary unemployment. To compute the 'probability of finding cultivation-related employment', therefore, we need data on involuntary unemployment *vis-a-vis cultivation-related work*. What is available, however, is data on involuntary unemployment vis-à-vis all (i.e. farm-related and nonfarm) work.

5 Labour Absorption by Cultivator Households

Introduction

John Kenneth Galbraith, commenting on the farm problem in *Economics Peace and Laughter* wrote, that 'A few liberals who knew about agriculture had for years been telling each other, and anyone else who would listen, that the truly forgotten man in farming was ... the hired farm worker. He added all the misfortunes of his employer to a specialized collection of his own'. It is to the demand for the primary resource of this 'forgotten man' that we now apply ourselves. Curiously, while a lot of research has been done on issues concerning the supply of labour both in the context of developing as well as developed agriculture, *relatively* little empirical evidence seems to be available on issues concerning the demand for hired labour. Empirical evidence on this, however, is important if we are to juxtapose it with the supply of wage labour in simultaneous equations analyses of the functioning of the labour market. In order to appreciate the difference between evidence relating to total labour use (on which some work is available) as distinct from hired labour use, consider the fact that the compulsions determining self-employment of *family* labour (that is, work on one's own farm) can be quite different from those influencing the employment of *hired* hands. In this chapter, therefore, we are specifically concerned with estimation of the demand for hired labour.

Formally, the hired labour market in rural India may be sub-divided into the irregular and regular labour markets (Binswanger *et.al.*, 1984; Walker and Ryan, 1990). The irregular labour market comprises the markets for daily casual labour and contract labour. The regular labour market comprises the markets for regular farm servants and domestic servants (Figure 5.1). Appraising evidence from the ICRISAT data set, Binswanger *et.al.* and Walker and Ryan report that the bulk of labour incomes are earned in the daily, casual labour market. Dreze and Mukherjee (1989), surveying studies pertaining to other regions of India as well, come to a similar conclusion that daily casual labour contracts are the 'most important' of all the contracts undertaken in the labour market. It is

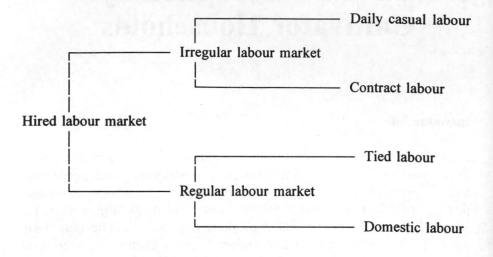

Figure 5.1 Rural labour markets in India

this segment of the market for hired labour that we study in this chapter, and unless otherwise stated hired labour shall refer to the daily rated or casual labour.

Even though the assertion that developing agriculture is a risky enterprise would not be considered controversial, these risks have not been explicitly accounted for in the received empirical studies of the demand for labour. Considering that production risk is inherent in much of developing agriculture in general and south Asian agriculture in particular, such incorporation is highly desirable. This chapter, therefore, is specifically concerned with the empirical estimation of the demand for hired labour under production risk. Given a downward-sloping demand for hired labour curve, rightward shifts in the supply of labour curve over time would imply increasing employment only at declining real wage rates (as in Figure 5.2a). In order that employment increases at nondecreasing (and preferably increasing) real wage rates over time, the demand for hired labour curve would have to exhibit appropriate rightward shifts (as in Figures 5.2b and 5.2c). What role does production risk play as a shifter of the demand for labour curve? A review of the theoretical literature on input demand under risk reveals that a marginal increase in risk will cause a *decline* in the demand for labour, given decreasing absolute risk aversion and a well-behaved production function (Batra and Ullah, 1974; Sandmo, 1971; Horowitz, 1970). If this decline were large enough, a positive price policy

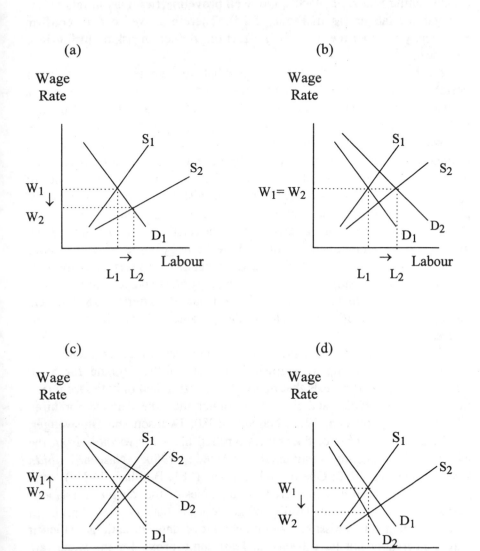

Figure 5.2 Alternative wage-employment combinations given shifts in the labour demand and supply curves over time

that is associated with an increasing variance of returns as in India (Hanumantha Rao *et.al.*, 1988) may well prove inefficacious in raising the demand for labour (as in Figure 5.2d). Therefore, we need to confirm empirically whether the (negative) effect of production risk on hiring-in is significant.

Furthermore, *given production risk*, what are the other important shifter variables of the demand for hired labour curve? A most interesting variable relevant in the Indian context is that of caste. While Bardhan (1984a) finds it to be a significant factor explaining hiring-in behaviour in eastern India, Binswanger *et.al.* (*ibid.*) and Walker and Ryan (*ibid.*) both find it to be unimportant in their samples from southern and western India. Moreover, in the context of a positive price policy being the cornerstone of agricultural policies in many developing (as also developed) countries, are price factors the important shifter variables? Or are the nonprice bio-chemical/mechanical innovations likely to be relatively important? Indeed, given that some components of the 'new technology' are expectedly labour displacing (such as chemical fertilisers as against manures), has the new technology *as a package* been labour displacing? (As an exception amongst studies dealing with this issue see Lipton and Longhurst, 1989; which, albeit, does not explicitly allude to the presence of risk in making its assessment).

A critique of the extant literature provides us with several additional reasons for undertaking an empirical analysis of the demand for hired labour under risk. It reveals that many studies estimated only the *total* (i.e. family plus hired) demand for labour rather than the demand for hired labour *per se* (Ishikawa, 1978; Naseem, 1980; Evenson and Binswanger, 1984). Secondly, some of the studies omitted the *wage variable* from the labour use function estimated (Ahmed, 1980; Naseem, *ibid.*; Wickramasekara, 1980; Oberoi and Ahmed, 1981; Bardhan, 1984a),[1] and hence may not even be considered to be studies of the *demand* for labour as such. Although the availability of appropriate data is often a problem (assuming that this omission was on account of data limitations, which it may conceivably not have been), at least some proxy for the wage rate should have been included rather than omit this variable altogether. Thirdly, the studies often failed to include other important regressors as well, as Bardhan (1984a) himself points out. Consequently, the specification bias is likely to be rather high in some of these studies, rendering hazardous the exercise of generalising on the basis of the reported results. Further, some of the studies used a productivity variable (variously defined) as a regressor, to capture the yield-enhancing and associated employment-generating potential of the changing technology (Ishikawa, *ibid.*; Naseem, *ibid.*). However, this variable is likely to be collinear with the input variables used in the demand functions estimated. Fourthly, most of the studies do not appear to be consistent with a farm household model of decision-making which, as we have argued, is the appropriate framework of analysis. While Evenson and Binswanger (*ibid.*) and Kalirajan and Shand (1982) base their estimations on the assumption of profit maximisation by farmers, in the presence of pervasive production risks a more appropriate framework of analysis might have been that of expected utility maximisation, especially since the latter subsumes the former as a possibility. Moreover, Kalirajan and Shand's elasticity estimates of hired labour with respect to the real wage rate (-1.5) and with respect to the real output price (2.5) appear to be quite out of line with the other available evidence for most of Asian agriculture. In our analysis of the demand for hired labour under risk we attempt to be mindful of all these shortcomings of the earlier studies.

A Model of the Demand for Labour

As we saw in chapter 3, the rural households in India may be categorised into cultivator households, landless households, and others (artisans, shopkeepers etc.). The present reality in much of south Asian agriculture is one where the first two groups predominate in terms of numbers, and the demand for hired labour arises mostly from the group of cultivator households. Consequently, the appropriate framework for analysing the demand for hired labour would be the farm household model. This we have already developed in detail in chapter 2. Recalling our analysis in chapter 2, we found that in the presence of production risk, the production and consumption decisions of the farm household are nonseparable. Consequently, the demand for labour (family plus hired) would be a function of the demographic variables, and we would have to solve for all the endogenous variables simultaneously. On account of the heavy data requirements associated with such an exercise, we considered it preferable to test for separability first. This would amount to testing if the demand for labour is significantly influenced by the demographic variables. For if it is not, separability may be justifiably assumed, and the demand for labour (as also the demand for *hired* labour *per se*) may be estimated independently of the other endogenous variables in the system. The unconditional reduced-form demand for labour function (on which the above-mentioned separability test is to be conducted), was derived as:

$$L = L \ (RWR, ROP, I, Z_1, Z_2, CVNR) \tag{2.13}$$

where all the variables are as defined previously.

Exogenous Factors Determining Labour Use

We now proceed to a detailed discussion of the exogenous factors determining labour use. Note that these factors, Z_1 and Z_2, appeared in the process of constructing the decision-theoretic model in chapter 2 above, and are not being added here *ex post*. At that point we had merely indicated what these factors could be, without going into a detailed discussion for the sake of continuity. What we intend to do here, therefore, is to spell out in detail how these factors influence the demand for labour, and how exactly we intend to measure them for purposes of empirical estimation. Keeping our data set in mind, we shall also point out if some of the theoretically relevant variables are likely to be relatively unimportant for our sample of households. The demand for labour is much more of a technical relationship as compared to the supply of labour. This follows from the fact that it is a 'derived demand', arising from the demand for the products that it enables to be produced. Pedagogically, the demand for labour may be seen to arise as a result of the complex interaction of several categories of technological and nontechnological factors.

Technological Factors

The first group of technological factors that we consider are those that are unambiguously labour-using in character. Irrigation is considered to be one of the most important factors inducing labour use (Vaidyanathan, 1980).[2] It does so in two ways, directly and indirectly. On the one hand, it induces labour use for the purpose of providing the irrigation itself, e.g. for flooding the furrows. On the other hand, it induces labour use indirectly as an enabling factor. Thus, it allows the extension of cultivated area, enables multiple cropping, leads to the extension of the effective cropping period and facilitates changes in the cropping pattern towards crops that are relatively labour-intensive. Further, it permits the use of chemical fertilisers and fertiliser-responsive high-yielding varieties of seeds (Lipton and Longhurst, *ibid.*). In order to properly assess the employment generation potential of this variable it may be important to account also for the type of irrigation in question. For instance, lift irrigation is relatively more labour-using than gravity-flow irrigation (Bardhan, 1978). Similarly, perennial, manipulable irrigation sources such as canals and tubewells may differ in their effect on labour use as compared to the relatively less dependable sources such as dug-wells and tanks (Bardhan, 1977). However, data on such detailed aspects may not be readily available. In trying to capture the effect of the irrigation variable note that it is partly land-augmenting in character. This may be captured by considering gross cropped area rather than the net sown area (see below for the discussion on the effect of farm size on the demand for labour). In addition irrigation also has an yield-augmenting aspect, which seems to have increased in importance in the context of the 'new technology'. This aspect is captured in terms of the percentage (cultivated) area irrigated.

Fertilisation and the use of modern high-yielding varieties of seeds will have a positive effect on labour use for the obvious reason that they are yield enhancing (Lipton and Longhurst, *ibid.*). Additional demand for labour may also be created for the negative reason that all fertilisers generally lead to the growth of weeds in addition to raising crop yields. Ishikawa (*ibid.*) points out that since farmyard manure is significantly more labour-intensive than chemical fertilisers, increased fertiliser *expenditure* need not imply increased labour use if it involves a substitution of chemical fertilisers for farmyard manures. It has been noticed that while the modern seed varieties may be used by themselves (although the consequent increase in yields may not be as much as it may be if these seeds are used in a package with the other modern inputs), it is detrimental to use chemical fertilisers in the absence of adequate supplies of water. This seems to have been the case in our sample villages where rainfall was unassured and the cropped area irrigated rather small. Thus, for instance, the mean fertilizer use in Shirapur was a mere two kg/hectare (Walker and Ryan, *ibid.*).

The second group of technological factors that we consider may *per se* be labour-saving in character, but in terms of their overall effect on (agricultural/rural) employment may well turn out to be labour-using. These factors are mainly farm implements and machines. Farm implements are seen to be more or less complementary to the labour input, reducing the drudge factor but not really displacing labour. The effect of mechanisation on labour demand creation, however, is a vexed and much-debated issue. For a detailed *a posteriori* analysis see Binswanger (1978).[3] It is difficult to say *a priori*, meanwhile, whether its overall effect on labour use is negative or positive. This partly depends on the particular operations that machines are used for. Thus, Bardhan (1977) notes that '... the direct employment effect of tractors would differ depending on how far they are used ... for the more labour-intensive operations like harvesting, drilling seeds, irrigation and transporting crops'. Indeed, by hastening the speed of certain operations the use of machines could effectively lengthen the cropping period. Ishikawa (1978) gives the example of Chinese agriculture where, he claims, the major impediment to the multiple cropping of rice in the Yangtze River Valley was the short cropping season of 120 days. But the use of pumps, threshers and tractors by hastening the harvesting and threshing of the first crop and the preparatory tilling and transplanting of the second, enabled the successful double cropping of rice. This led to commensurate increments in the demand for labour. In our sample villages, however, the use of implements and machines (especially tractors) is minimal (Walker and Ryan, *ibid.*). All of these inputs complementary to labour, such as fertilisers, high yielding seed varieties, farm implements etc., have been allowed for by including input expenditure as a regressor. It is probably preferable to lump together the expenditures on these inputs, because we would like to assess their effect on labour demand as a package.

The third category of technological factors that we consider are 'institutional conditions' that may be peculiar to a region (Ishikawa, *ibid.*). Thus, unusual climatic and soil characteristics may necessitate the use of large amounts of labour. For instance, the high clay content of the soils of the Saga Plains in Japan made tilling relatively difficult, thereby inducing increased (draught, and hence, human) labour use. Similarly, the peculiar topography of a region may induce high labour use. The fields in the Saga Plains being higher than the creeks from which water was raised for irrigating them, exceptionally high labour use became necessary for lifting the water and bunding the fields to prevent its leakage. Such factors may be taken as given for a given sample region. Alternatively, they may be thought of as influencing the overall average effect of the regressors on the regressand. In other words, the effect of such factors may be picked up via the intercept term. Since our sample villages were purposively selected to reflect the diverse agroclimatic and edaphic characteristics of their respective regions, we capture these inter-regional differences by allowing for a separate intercept term for each village.

A somewhat different class of 'institutional' issues relates to the effect of tenancy on labour use. The argument made is that tenancy (that is, sharecropping not fixed rent tenancy) leads to suboptimal productivity and a suboptimal labour input because the tenant stands to receive only a part of his marginal product of labour. Similar incentive problems also arise regarding the use of other production inputs, including investments into land improvement. Consequently, tenancy may be said to lead to depressed labour use in this indirect manner as well (for the improvements in land may have led to a higher labour demand). There is a large literature discussing the theoretical intricacies of tenancy related issues (Singh, 1989). From the viewpoint of our analysis, however, the important question is whether tenancy was a significant enough phenomenon in our sample villages. Jodha (1984) looks at the incidence of tenancy in the ICRISAT villages (including Aurepalle, Kanzara, and Shirapur) over the time period 1975-76/78-79. He finds that the area transferred *on account of tenancy per se* as a percentage of the total operated area of the sample households was only 12% in Aurepalle and 15% in Kanzara annually. Only in Shirapur was this proportion large, approximating 41% annually. Moreover, points out Jodha, in Aurepalle more than 76% of the leased area had fixed rent contracts, although the corresponding figure for Kanzara was much smaller at 17% and insignificant for Shirapur at 1%. In another study of these very villages over the longer time span 1975-76/82-83, Shaban (1985) confirms the above findings even more strongly. He finds that share tenancy was prevalent on only 0.5% of the cropped area in Aurepalle, 12% of the cropped area in Kanzara and about 36% of the cropped area in Shirapur. Finally, note that in our sample, 40 out of the total of 53 households (or more than three-fourths) were from Aurepalle and Kanzara. Therefore, for most of the households in our sample tenancy was probably not an important factor in determining labour use.

Yet another class of institutional issues relates to the effect of tied labour on casual labour use. Hired labour, we noted above, may also comprise 'regular farm servants'. This is also called 'tied' labour or 'permanent' labour as it is bound to the employers by relatively long term contracts. Richards (1979) argued that tied labour was really a way of supervising casual labour. Bardhan (1979b) suggested that landlords would offer permanent contracts in the 'lean season' in order to avoid recruitment costs and ensure the availability of labour in the 'peak season'. Alternatively, Bardhan (1983) averred that an uncertain expected wage would induce risk averse labourers to opt for permanent contracts with risk neutral landlords. Pal (1996) extends the earlier work by arguing that the choice between permanent and casual contracts also depends on the time and credit constraints of workers, and not just the wage rate. Eswaran and Kotwal (1985) hypothesize that permanent contracts are actually attempts to 'convert' hired into family labour in order to reduce supervision costs. Whatever the explanation for the use of tied labour, the implication is that tied labour is one of the factors determining casual labour use by farm households.

There may be reason to believe, however, that tied labour may not have been necessary to supervise the casual labour *a la* Richards, or to transform it into family labour *a la* Eswaran and Kotwal, in our sample villages. For, using ICRISAT data, Battese *et.al.* (1989) show that there was no significant difference in productivity between family labour and hired hands. But this result may be discounted by arguing that the productivity of hired labour in the Battese sample was measured *given the positive effect of the tied labour used* by the households on the productivity of hired labour. In our sample villages, however, the use of permanent labour was never widespread. Binswanger *et.al.* (1984; Tables 8.2, 8.3) report that only 11 individuals in Aurepalle, 10 in Shirapur and Kalman, and 24 in Kanzara and Kinkheda were employed as permanent labourers. Assuming that all the permanent labour was employed by the cultivator households (of which there were 29 in Aurepalle, 55 in Shirapur/Kalman, and 59 in Kanzara/Kinkheda in the Binswanger *et.al.* study), about 62% of the cultivator households in Aurepalle, 82% in Shirapur/Kalman and 59% in Kanzara/Kinkheda *did not* employ a permanent labourer. If we allow for the fact that tied labour is most likely employed by large farmers (Walker and Ryan, *ibid.*, p. 111), of which there was a disproportionately small number in our sample, the proportion of farm households in our sample not having any permanent labour would be even larger. This appears to be even truer of the early-1980s or the latter half of our sample period, because the supply of such labour tightened considerably over this period (Walker and Ryan, *ibid.*, p. 133). In view of this evidence it appears that the empirical importance of this variable as a determinant of the demand for casual labour was rather limited for our sample.

Nontechnological Factors

The factors determining the demand for labour are not entirely technological in nature. The demand for labour may also depend on demographic variables. Thus, it may depend on the family size of the households demanding the labour — larger households perhaps requiring less labour. Additionally, the age and sex composition of the family should also be important. These variables were proxied by the number of prime age males, number of prime age females, number of elderly dependent males and number of elderly dependent females in the family; where the prime age group is defined as 15-55 years and those above 55 are considered elderly dependents (Benjamin, 1992). The larger the number of prime age members the larger would be the capacity, although the less the need, to hire outside help. The larger the number of dependents, the larger would be the need to hire outside help.

The households' resources, land and nonland, would be another determinant of the demand for labour. The effect of farm size on the demand for (hired) labour is expected to be positive, smaller farms usually being more dependent on family labour. To allow for increases in cropping intensity and other land-augmenting changes over time, the farm size concept that is relevant here is gross cropped area rather than net sown area. The magnitude of nonland resources would partially determine the productivity of the land base and, by providing collateral, also determine the household's command over the complementary inputs into production. So that one would expect larger nonland resources to induce a larger demand for labour.

The older the working family members the more difficult would it be for them to provide the labour requisite for doing the on-farm chores. Consequently, the higher would be the demand for labour. This factor may be proxied by the age of the household head, who is assumed to be the *de facto* decision-maker. Another relevant household characteristic would be the education of the members. What effect this will have on the demand for labour is not immediately clear. If those with higher schooling try to earn the rewards for their higher potential marginal products by working off-farm, then higher education in the family will lead to a higher demand for labour. This effect will tend to get reinforced if, as Bardhan (1984b) suggests, the educated tend to be averse to manual labour. If, however, it is not possible to work off-farm for whatever reason (say, lack of appropriate labour market opportunities), then a higher education may not translate into a higher demand for labour. The education variable may be proxied by the number of years of formal education of the household head. This may not be completely satisfactory, since the average level of farmers' education is likely to be minimal in less developed countries (see chapter 3). A more well-defined measure of the farmers' exposure to 'logical open thinking', attributes that are ascribed to formal education, is necessary. However, how such an index should be computed is not quite obvious, forcing us to fall back on the number of years of formal education (of the household head) as a rather imperfect proxy.

Finally, the household's caste may be an important determinant of the demand for labour. For if the household belongs to a 'high' caste, its members may be unwilling to do menial and/or manual work. It may then have to hire outside help on its farm. We represent the household's caste status by an index based on its religious, social and economic status, prepared by Doherty, a social anthropologist (see chapter 3).

Having discussed the exogenous variables Z_1 and Z_2, we complete the discussion of the regressors in equation (2.13) by noting that the real daily wage rate (RWR) for each household is estimated by dividing the wage bill by the number of labour days hired, and then deflating this ratio by the (weighted average) exogenous price of the market purchased good.

Model Specification and Estimation Results

We first test for the separation hypothesis. As explained above (as well as in chapter 2), this consists of testing whether the demographic variables are significant determinants of the total household demand for labour (i.e. hired plus family labour). Only if separation holds would we be justified in estimating the 'production side' of the system separately from the 'consumption side'. In that case, we proceed with the estimation of the demand for hired labour, since that is what we are primarily interested in. Finally, we also estimate the total demand for labour (family plus hired) *per acre*, in order to test for the inverse relationship between farm size and productivity in the presence of production risk.

It would be preferable to estimate the demand functions by pooling the cross section and time series observations. There are several ways of doing so. One such simple method used in the literature is the fixed effects model where we use dummy variables for each of the sample villages. We prefer using village-specific dummies rather than household-specific dummies, because the households residing in a particular village face a more or less similar environment, whereas this is not true across the villages (see chapter 3). This amounts to using a separate intercept term for each of the three villages. Recall from our discussion of the exogenous factors above that we had decided to use village dummies to represent the diverse soil and agroclimatic features of the sample villages. Thus, these dummies serve the twin purpose of capturing the diverse soil and agroclimatic characteristics of the villages as well as pooling the cross section and time series observations. The 'dummy variables model' may then be written as:

$$L = \Sigma_j\ \beta_{1j}D_{jt} + \Sigma_{k=2}^{K}\ \beta_k X_{kit} + v_{it} \qquad\qquad (5.1)$$

where L is, in alternative regressions, the total demand for labour, the demand for hired labour and the total demand for labour per acre; vector X is the set of regressors (RWR, ROP, Z_1, Z_2, and $CVNR$);[4] errors $v_{it} \sim NIID(0, \sigma^2)$; and D_{jt} are dummy variables such that $D_{jt} = 1$ if $j = i$ and 0 otherwise. Subscript t refers to the sample period, and $i, j = 1, 2, 3$ for Aurepalle, Shirapur and Kanzara, respectively. The results, for the three alternative dependent variables, are presented in Tables 5.1 to 5.3.

Alternatively, we may pool the data via more complicated assumptions about the error terms for the different households and time periods, as in the cross-sectionally heteroscedastic time-wise autoregressive model (Kmenta, 1986). Estimation results using this specification are reported in Tables 5.4 to 5.6 for the different dependent variables. The estimation of complicated cross section-time series models as Kmenta's, however, often runs into practical problems. Thus, while the results in Table 5.4 are based on a 'fully' cross-sectionally heteroscedastic time-wise autoregressive specification, the results in Tables 5.5 and 5.6 are perforce based on a specification where the autoregression parameter had to be restricted to be the same for each household, for otherwise the software used (see White, 1993) was unable to invert the design matrix. Furthermore, the number of regressors for each household is too large in comparison to the length of the time series, so that the divisor used by the software in estimating the variances is T (the number of observations on each cross section) rather than $T - K$ (the degrees of freedom for each cross section). This introduces a downward bias in the standard errors and an upward bias in the t-statistics. Another problem with using the 'full' or Kmenta model is that its asymptotic properties depend on both T and N (the number of cross sections) being large (Kmenta, *ibid.*). Therefore, when T is small (as in our case), we should take note of the small sample biases of such pooled estimators whose asymptotic properties depend on T being large. Finally, note that the results from the simpler dummy variables or fixed effects specification (Tables 5.1 to 5.3) are virtually the same as those of the more complicated 'full' specification (Tables 5.4 to 5.6). Since we lose nothing in using the former, our discussion below shall be based on results from the dummy variables model.[5]

The least squares estimates of the *total* demand for labour (i.e. hired plus family labour) are given in Table 5.1. Note that all the household composition variables — family size (FS), prime age males (PAM), prime age females (PAF), elderly dependent males (EDM) and elderly dependent females (EDF) — are statistically insignificant. A likelihood ratio test for the joint insignificance of these variables cannot be rejected at even the

Table 5.1 Total demand for labour: dummy variables model, OLS estimates

Variable	Regression coefficient	T-value 459 d.o.f	Elasticity at means
RWR	-51.046	-3.972	-0.22
ROP	139.590	3.131	0.26
AGE	2.131	2.100	0.31
EDU	8.369	3.169	0.07
CASTE	-9.419	-2.253	-0.08
FS	1.938	0.397	0.04
PAM	-0.300	-0.030	-0.002
PAF	-14.038	-1.337	-0.08
EDM	-2.719	-0.139	-0.003
EDF	-12.802	-0.600	-0.01
GCA	15.038	22.510	0.75
PAIRR	4.720	10.270	0.15
INEXP	0.010	2.980	0.05
NLASS	0.006	6.150	0.20
CVNR	-0.188	-0.457	0.00
D1	-143.730	-2.513	-0.15
D2	-307.160	-5.559	-0.22
D3	-56.630	-1.090	-0.07

$\bar{R}^2$ = 0.8245

Number of observations = 477

LR statistic (FS = PAM = PAF = EDM = EDF = 0) = 2.74

LR statistic (all slope coefficients = 0) = 821.34

10% level (the *LR* test statistic being 2.74 as compared to the 10% critical value of χ^2 (5 degrees of freedom) = 9.24). In other words, the null hypothesis of separation is upheld. This justifies the estimation of the 'production' and 'consumption' sides of the farm household model separately. Now, within the total demand for labour, what interests us more is the demand for hired labour *per se*. And this is what we estimate next. Note, in passing, that the significance of the household composition variables in the demand for *hired* labour function does *not* constitute a test of the separation hypothesis.

Table 5.2 Demand for hired labour: dummy variables model, OLS estimates

Variable	Regression coefficient	T-value 459 dof	Elasticity at means
RWR	−47.135	−3.907	−0.30
ROP	46.810	1.119	0.13
AGE	1.522	1.598	0.33
EDU	14.814	5.975	0.17
CASTE	−5.553	−1.415	−0.07
FS	5.011	1.094	0.15
PAM	−17.277	−1.849	−0.14
PAF	−42.431	−4.306	−0.36
EDM	−34.433	−1.877	−0.05
EDF	−0.871	−0.044	−0.001
GCA	13.068	20.840	0.95
PAIRR	3.381	7.834	0.16
INEXP	0.010	3.051	0.07
NLASS	0.005	5.311	0.24
CVNR	−0.228	−0.590	0.00
D1	−39.535	−0.736	−0.06
D2	−201.260	−3.880	−0.21
D3	−4.034	−0.083	−0.01

$\bar{R}^2 = 0.8013$

Number of observations = 477

LR statistic (all slope coefficients = 0) = 760.26

The least squares estimates of the demand for *hired* labour are presented in Table 5.2. The real wage rate for hired labour (RWR) is found to have a highly significant negative effect on the demand for hired labour, the associated elasticity 'at the means' being −0.30. The real output price (ROP) has an insignificant effect on the regressand. If at all it was felt that offering increasingly higher product prices would not only raise agricultural production and productivity but also lead to significant increases in the demand for hired labour in the process, our results show that such a supposition was probably unfounded, atleast for the crops grown by our sample households (in which the staples sorghum and millets predominated,

Table 5.3 Total demand for labour per acre: dummy variables model, OLS estimates

Variable	Regression coefficient	T-value 459 dof	Elasticity at means
RWR	−1.103	−1.434	−0.08
ROP	6.256	2.345	0.19
AGE	0.020	0.330	0.05
EDU	0.237	1.501	0.03
CASTE	−0.540	−2.157	−0.07
FS	0.122	0.416	0.04
PAM	0.366	0.614	0.03
PAF	−0.935	−1.489	−0.08
EDM	−1.300	−1.111	−0.02
EDF	−2.672	−2.093	−0.03
GCA	−0.216	−5.408	−0.17
PAIRR	0.378	13.730	0.19
INEXP	0.0001	0.605	0.01
NLASS	0.0002	2.816	0.09
CVNR	0.019	0.762	0.00
D1	15.811	4.618	0.25
D2	10.448	3.159	0.12
D3	23.839	7.666	0.46

$\bar{R}^2 = 0.4866$

Number of observations = 477

LR statistic (FS = PAM = PAF = EDM = EDF = 0) = 7.96

LR statistic (all slope coefficients = 0) = 263.76

and the other important crops were rice, cotton and castor). Both the age (AGE) and the education (EDU) levels of the household head have a positive effect on the demand for hired labour, with the latter highly significant at the 1% level. The latter relationship appears to be consistent with Bardhan's explanation that relatively educated individuals probably develop an aversion to manual labour, necessitating hiring-in by the farm household. The number of prime age males (PAM) and prime age females (PAF) in the household negatively affect the dependent variable, both being significant statistically. Interestingly, the elderly dependent males (EDM) variable is also significantly negatively related to the regressand. This could mean that some of those who fall in this category *a priori* are actually working on their own farms and hence substitute for hired labour. The caste variable (CASTE) is found to be insignificantly related to the hiring-in of labour. This confirms Binswanger *et.al.*'s (*ibid.*) and Walker and Ryan's (*ibid.*) observation, that in the daily casual labour market in south-central India caste is unimportant as a determinant of who hires whom. This evidence is contrary to that of Bardhan (1984a) for eastern India, who found that in rural West Bengal the upper caste households' aversion to manual work leads to a relatively higher demand for hired labour. Gross cropped area (GCA) exercises a very strong positive influence on the hiring-in of labour, the associated elasticity being as high as 0.95. Similarly, the percentage area irrigated (PAIRR) also exercises a strong positive influence on hiring-in, although the associated elasticity is a modest 0.16. The expenditure on variable inputs (INEXP) — which mostly comprised expenditure on seeds, chemical fertilisers and manures, and implements and machinery — has a positive and significant effect on the demand for hired labour. However, the associated elasticity of 0.07 is rather small. Higher nonland assets (NLASS) increase the hiring-in of labour, the associated elasticity being a reasonable 0.24. Production risk appears to have an insignificant effect on the demand for hired labour — with the (conditional) coefficient of variation of net revenue (CVNR) being statistically insignificant. Finally, of the intercept dummies (*D1*, *D2* and *D3*), that for village Shirapur (*D2*) has a significant negative effect on hiring-in. This is quite understandable given that the agroclimatic and soil characteristics of Shirapur were such as to make it relatively drought prone and risky in comparison to the other two villages. This would naturally make for a lower hiring-in potential.

There exists a large literature which has explored the inverse relationship between farm size and its productivity and found one of the important reasons for this phenomenon to be the relatively higher labour use per acre on the smaller farms. This explanation, in turn, has been based on the argument that the opportunity cost of family labour is relatively lower for the small farmers on account of the constraints imposed on the off-farm labour supply of female (and child) labour in the farm household (see, for instance, Bardhan, 1973). Therefore, since the implicit labour cost works out to be lower on the smaller farms according to this argument, such farms tend to apply more labour per acre than the larger farms. With overall development over time, economic as well as non-economic, it would be of interest to test if the above-mentioned constraints on female

Table 5.4 Total demand for labour: full model*, OLS estimates

Variable	Regression coefficient	T-value 459 dof	Elasticity at means
RWR	−18.084	−3.170	−0.08
ROP	83.659	4.388	0.16
AGE	0.954	1.787	0.14
EDU	8.507	3.855	0.07
CASTE	−5.601	−3.248	−0.05
FS	−1.065	−0.377	−0.02
PAM	7.656	1.344	0.04
PAF	−6.541	−0.963	−0.04
EDM	−5.630	−0.406	−0.01
EDF	−2.877	−0.225	−0.002
GCA	13.748	23.120	0.69
PAIRR	3.619	11.670	0.12
INEXP	0.003	1.742	0.01
NLASS	0.007	6.760	0.24
CVNR	0.076	0.554	0.00
D1	−103.930	−3.489	−0.10
D2	−220.200	−6.597	−0.16
D3	−31.696	−1.211	−0.04

* Cross-sectionally heteroscedastic time-wise autoregressive model
Buse R^2 = 0.7999
Number of observations = 477
LR statistic (FS = PAM = PAF = EDM = EDF = 0) = 0.06
LR statistic (all slopes = 0) = 93.86

labour supply have weakened enough to have equalised labour use per acre on farms of different sizes. This we do by running a regression of the demand for labour per acre on farm size, while controlling for the wage rate and other explanatory factors. The regression results given in Table 5.3 reveal that the total demand for labour per acre is negatively and significantly related to the farm size variable. Extrapolating from this result, if a higher demand for labour per acre may be assumed to indicate a higher land productivity, the inverse relationship between farm size and productivity may still be expected to hold in these semi-arid tracts, despite

Table 5.5 Demand for hired labour: full model*, OLS estimates

Variable	Regression coefficient	T-value 459 dof	Elasticity at means
RWR	−9.111	−2.012	−0.06
ROP	6.768	0.452	0.02
AGE	0.011	0.020	0.002
EDU	11.387	5.318	0.13
CASTE	−2.810	−1.846	−0.04
FS	1.783	0.606	0.05
PAM	2.375	0.423	0.02
PAF	−29.312	−4.940	−0.25
EDM	0.330	0.026	0.001
EDF	−8.152	−0.625	−0.01
GCA	10.077	18.320	0.74
PAIRR	1.817	6.833	0.09
INEXP	0.002	1.902	0.02
NLASS	0.005	6.651	0.27
CVNR	0.044	0.229	0.00
D1	−9.098	−0.204	−0.01
D2	−114.330	−3.227	−0.12
D3	29.356	0.979	0.05

* Cross sectionally heteroscedastic time-wise autoregressive model
Buse R^2 = 0.6950
LR statistic (all slopes = 0) = 28.46

economic development and a more comprehensive specification (of the demand function) that allows for production risk.

Conclusions

In situations of abysmally low standards of living as in the rural developing country setup, one would not like to see an increase in employment at the cost of the real wage rate. But that is exactly what would happen with rightward shifts of the labour supply curve over time, given a downward sloping labour demand curve, as for our sample of households, *unless* the

Table 5.6 Total demand for labour per acre: full model[*], OLS estimates

Variable	Regression coefficient	T-value 459 dof	Elasticity at means
RWR	−0.375	−0.742	−0.03
ROP	1.323	0.754	0.04
AGE	0.003	0.060	0.01
EDU	0.204	1.351	0.03
CASTE	−0.231	−1.527	−0.03
FS	0.010	0.041	0.003
PAM	0.673	1.345	0.06
PAF	−0.302	−0.611	−0.03
EDM	0.477	0.499	0.01
EDF	−2.049	−2.013	−0.03
GCA	−0.171	−6.323	−0.13
PAIRR	0.317	11.890	0.16
INEXP	0.0001	0.570	0.005
NLASS	0.0001	3.023	0.08
CVNR	0.006	0.661	0.00
D1	15.715	5.341	0.25
D2	9.172	3.417	0.11
D3	22.958	8.268	0.45

[*] Cross sectionally heteroscedastic time-wise autoregressive model
Buse R^2 = 0.5467
LR statistic (FS = PAM = PAF = EDM = EDF = 0) = 4.64
LR statistic (all slopes = 0) = 99.84

labour demand curve also exhibits appropriate rightward shifts. The situation would become serious if, instead, there were factors at work with a tendency to shift the labour demand curve *to the left*. Indeed, the theoretical literature on input demand under production risk shows that a marginal increase in production risk would cause a *decline* in the demand for labour. Therefore, it becomes important to test whether this negative effect is statistically significant. We find that an increase in production risk, i.e. the (conditional) coefficient of variation of net revenue has an insignificant effect on the demand for hired labour. This is an important result. A number of studies have noted that the use of the 'new technology' has led not only to increased production levels but also increased yield and revenue variability (see, for instance, Hanumantha Rao *et.al*, 1988, in the Indian context). Our results reveal that this increase in variability associated with the use of the new technology, whatever be its other shortcomings, probably does not have any significant negative effect on the demand for hired labour. Similarly, we do not find the caste variable to be significantly related to the demand for hired labour. This contradicts Bardhan's (1984a) finding for eastern India where upper caste households' aversion to manual labour led to a higher demand for hired labour. Our result supports the observation of Binswanger *et.al.* (*ibid.*) and Walker and Ryan (*ibid.*) that, in general, caste was an unimportant determinant of who hired whom in the villages of south-central India.

Nonprice technological factors turn out to be the relatively important shifter variables of the demand curve. Very generally, this accords with the results of earlier studies which, albeit, did not account for the presence of production risk in their empirical estimations. One of the most important factors is the gross cropped area, with an elasticity of 0.95. Since the physical quantity of land cannot be increased by any appreciable extent in the Asian context in general and the Indian context in particular, this result points towards the importance of land-augmenting technological change. For instance, irrigation, fertilisers and even some kinds of machinery for certain operations allow marginal land to be brought under the plough, extend the effective cropping period, permit appropriate changes in the cropping pattern, and enable multiple cropping. Thus, the percentage area irrigated is found to significantly increase hiring-in, the elasticity of response being 0.16; although it should be realised that the land-augmenting aspect of this variable has been subsumed in the gross cropped area variable, as explained earlier. Second, nonland assets is a fairly important shifter variable with a reasonably high elasticity of 0.24. This factor would ultimately determine how intensively the land asset can be utilised by the household. Further, rural employment need not be related to crop husbandry alone but may also relate to animal husbandry, repairs and maintenance, building and construction etc. Naturally, larger nonland assets would imply a larger employment potential in these activities. Finally, even though the elasticity associated with input expenditure is very small, its significantly positive effect on hiring-in is meaningful. It implies that the *package* of modern technology utilised has been labour using and not labour displacing. This supports the conclusion reached by Lipton and Longhurst (*ibid.*), although their analysis did not take account of production risk. This result is important because sometimes the debate on labour use in the context of the new technology has gone off on a tangent and has restricted itself to testing whether a specific input, say chemical fertilisers, is labour using or labour displacing. What is more relevant, on the contrary, is whether the entire package of new inputs used has been labour using or not in the net.

Notes

1 Only the 1956-57 cross section regression for Hooghly district does not contain the wage variable in Bardhan (1984a).
2 In the course of highlighting and critiquing the discussion that occurred at a series of seminars on labour absorption in agriculture, organised under the auspices of the Asian Regional Team for Employment Promotion, at one point Vaidyanathan comments that 'It should be added that our current knowledge *does not permit us to go beyond saying* that irrigation increases labour absorption ...' (Vaidyanathan, 1980, p.284, italics ours). While it may be too strong to aver that this is all we can state with confidence presently, it serves to underscore the importance of irrigation in generating agricultural employment.
3 Binswanger's conclusions cannot necessarily be extrapolated to different economic environs as he himself carefully points out: '*In a different environment ... the introduction of tractors must be expected to lead to different results*' (p. 1; italics in the original).
4 Variable *I* (exogenous income) had to be omitted for lack of data. Given the small proportion that this constitutes in total household income (see Walker and Ryan, 1990), this omission is not likely to be important.
5 It might have been more appropriate to include time dummies in the models estimated. However, we found that including time dummies left the results unchanged as to coefficient signs and their significance, as well as   etc., but the caste variable now had a counter-intuitive sign in the demand for hired labour regression   it was *negative* and significant. One would expect this variable either to have a positive sign (as Bardhan argues) or else be insignificant (as noted by Binswanger *et.al.*, 1984, and Walker and Ryan, 1990, for the ICRISAT villages). But a negative and significant sign does not make sense. In the event, we felt that including time dummies was an improvement only on paper and was best eschewed.

6 The Hiring-Out Behaviour of Rural Households

Introduction

There is a saying in the *Old Testament* that 'A worker's appetite works on his behalf, his hungry mouth drives him on'. To paraphrase, the supply of labour is determined by a worker's need. And the influence of production risk often makes this need more acute. Our point of departure in this monograph was the observation that a potentially important variable which continues to be overlooked in *empirical* analyses of farmers' off-farm labour supply is risk. The reference, as our subsequent analysis expatiated, was primarily to production risk. The *theoretical* labour supply literature, relating both to the individual consumer and the farm household under risk, has had few unambiguous results to present. While the theoretical studies can sign some comparative-static responses for 'additive risk', they are unable to do so for 'multiplicative risk' (Block and Heineke, 1973; Dardanoni, 1988). Despite rather simple analytical frameworks, the results from these studies hinge critically on the third derivative properties of the utility function. Since we have no strong priors about these derivatives, assumptions relating to them are themselves testable hypotheses. If we were to extend the analytical models in these studies to allow for endogenous income and a multiple argument utility function (as in a farm household production model, for instance), even the additive risk results may become open to question. Empirically, therefore, we can remove some of these ambiguities without necessarily having to make equally limiting assumptions. Specifically, we can test whether an increase in revenue risk will increase, decrease or leave unchanged the off-farm supply of labour by farmers.

Closely related to the above question is the issue whether some mechanism exists which allows the farm household to adjust to increases in revenue uncertainty. This would be especially pertinent for developing country farmers for whom such risks are likely to be pronounced in the face of relatively imperfect insurance, capital and futures markets. Does the farm household hedge against production uncertainty by varying its off-farm labour supply? The answer to this query would also be useful for understanding the broader implications of price stabilisation schemes (for agricultural commodities), although such issues do not concern us in this monograph and need to be taken up separately. Briefly, therefore, producers in developing agriculture may be significant suppliers of labour as well, because their land base is too small and unproductive to employ all of their family labour. The impact of stabilisation policies, hence, should be analysed not only in terms of efficiency gains and changes in producer revenues from on-farm production (Newbery and Stiglitz, 1981), but also in terms of their effect on off-farm labour income. Even though off-farm labour income is of secondary importance to producers (for whom cultivation is the major occupation, by definition), the effect of commodity price stabilisation (or risk reduction) on labour incomes may be significant and may swamp the effect on efficiency gains and revenue from self-cultivation.

Finally, there arises the question whether the inclusion of risk in labour supply models will alter the relationships of the other explanatory variables to the hiring out of labour. For instance, it would be of interest to note the off-farm labour supply response with respect to the wage rate. Bardhan (1979a) finds a significantly *negative* wage response for his sample of cultivators in rural India. Rosenzweig (1980) reports a similar result for another Indian sample of male farmers. Although for women he reports a significant *positive* relation, considering the overwhelming proportion of males in the agricultural labour force, we would also expect an inverse association between *total* (male plus female) off-farm labour supply and the wage rate. Could the omission of risk variables have biased the wage response of off-farm labour supply by an amount large enough to change its sign?

Our analysis of the previous empirical work on off-farm labour allocation in chapter 2 showed, that most of the studies had not allowed for the presence of any kind of risk, and specifically production risk. The few that did, had done so rather inadequately. Furthermore, none of the studies raised the set of issues that we mentioned in the preceding paragraphs. Therefore, in an attempt to address these issues we developed in chapter 2 estimable models of market labour supply beginning from a static farm household model under production risk. The unconditional reduced form function for desired off-farm labour supply by cultivator households was shown to be

$$F_2^* = F_2^* (ERWR, ROP, I, Z_1, Z_2, CVNR) \tag{2.14}$$

and the reduced form function for desired off-farm labour supply by landless households was shown to be

$$F_2^* = F_2^* \text{ (ERWR, I, } Z_1, \text{ AVCVNR)} \tag{2.15}$$

where all the variables are as defined previously. Equation (2.14), we argued, could be estimated by itself only if the farm household production model could be shown to be separable. In chapter 5 we tested for separability, and found that the household production model may indeed be taken to be separable for our sample of cultivators. Therefore, the supply of off-farm labour by cultivator households may be estimated independently of the other endogenous variables in the system. There was no such problem of separability to be taken care of in the case of landless households, so that equation (2.15) could in any case be estimated by itself. It is to the estimation of these functions that we turn in this chapter.

Exogenous Factors Determining Off-farm Labour Supply

We now discuss in detail the exogenous factors, Z_1 and Z_2, included in the labour supply equations to be estimated. Although this task has been simplified because we have already discussed in the previous chapter how the various exogenous variables affect the *demand* for labour, we still need to spell out how these variables may influence the *hiring-out* of labour, especially since the direction of causation may be *a priori* ambiguous.

An important factor determining off-farm labour supply is the gross cropped area. The larger the area under cultivation, ceteris paribus, the heavier the requirements on the household's labour time and, hence, the less the hiring-out of labour. While this variable accounts for the multiple cropping that irrigation can afford, it does not capture the yield-enhancing effect of irrigation. The latter may be captured by the percentage (gross cropped) area irrigated. Similarly, other components of the 'new technology' such as fertilisation, high-yielding seed varieties and the use of machinery and implements can be yield increasing, thereby discouraging off-farm labour supply. This effect may be captured in terms of the total input expenditure. The nonland assets of a household delimit the scope for the utilisation of the available land and hence determine its production potential. Thus, we would expect a larger nonland assets base to discourage off-farm labour supply.

In view of the typically impoverished assets base of rural households in developing agriculture, another important set of factors determining hiring-out would be those relating to family size and composition. The larger the family size, ceteris paribus, the greater would be the supply of wage labour. But given the different social valuation of male and female work (more on this below), hiring-out may be differentially affected by the number of prime age males and prime age females in the family. Further, the pressure to hire out would vary depending on the number of elderly dependent males and elderly dependent females in the family.

With regard to the working members in the household, it is often held that the older the worker the more experienced he is likely to be. But given that entrepreneurial ability cannot be hired out, we would expect a negative relationship between hiring-out and age. To the extent that a higher age also implies debility and hence lower productivity, a negative relationship between hiring-out and age may be further strengthened. An important factor in determining a farmer's entrepreneurial ability is his education, which is usually measured in terms of the number of years of formal education of the household head. How this factor influences hiring-out behaviour is difficult to hypothesize *a priori*. To the extent that education increases the marginal product of labour in the present occupation or improves entrepreneurial and managerial skills, we would expect it to have a negative relation to off-farm labour supply. However, to the extent that the returns to the potentially higher marginal product may be realized only from the higher paying alternatives to farming, it may induce increased hiring-out.

A rather important factor in the rural Indian context is caste. There is much evidence to show that many occupations were traditionally determined along caste lines and continue to be so. This fact may be especially important for women given that extra-mural labour by them, at least in certain occupations, is not considered very respectable; so that women of the higher caste households may be discouraged from seeking off-farm employment. We must note also that the caste variable is somewhat fuzzy insofar as it relates to the overall position of the household in the social hierarchy which, in turn, may be a function of social, economic and religious factors. We saw in chapter 3, that a caste index which accounts for these varied aspects is Doherty's index. Finally, the different villages in our sample were selected with the express purpose of representing the diverse agroclimatic and soil conditions of the semi-arid tropical regions under study. We propose to pick this up in terms of a separate intercept term for each village.

The Regressand

The regressand in our model is supposed to be the *desired* supply of labour, for we have considered the issue of labour supply response from the viewpoint of the supplier. In the absence of any demand constraints the actual labour days supplied by the households would also constitute their desired supply. Given the presence of unemployment, however, Ham (1982) finds that the use of actual days of work in estimation leads to inconsistent parameter estimates. Traditionally, a variety of approaches have been adopted to redress this problem. Some researchers simply assume that the workers are not constrained in their choice. Others argue that unemployment actually represents leisure. Alternatively, one may argue that the constrained workers are only a small part of the sample, but this, of course, is an empirical question. A different approach is to remove the underemployed (Wales and Woodland, 1976, 1977), or the unemployed (Da Vanzo, de Tray and Greenberg, 1976) from the sample. Heckman (1979) shows, however, that if the probability of being underemployed or unemployed is correlated with the error term or any of the regressors, this technique will yield inconsistent parameter estimates. Finally, Ham (1980) explicitly introduced an upper bound on the labour that could be supplied by the workers. But, as he points out, this would lead to inconsistent estimates if the constraint is not binding.

In the context of our sample, we are fortunate in that we have information not merely on which workers were unemployed, but also on the number of days for which they were (involuntarily) unemployed. The question asked of the respondents in our survey was: 'On how many days since the last interview (a period of 2-3 weeks) were you available and/or looking for work, and failed to find any'? The desired off-farm labour supply is then derived as the sum of the actual number of labour days worked by the households and the number of days of involuntary unemployment. In the following section we analyse the total household labour supply from the cultivator households.

Estimation of Off-Farm Labour Supply

Given that the dependent variable in our models is censored, one method of estimation would be the tobit maximum likelihood procedure. This method, however, is overly restrictive in that it hypothesizes the *direction* of influence of a given regressor on the *probability* of participation to be the same as the *direction* of influence of that regressor on the *extent* of participation in the labour market. In actual fact these two effects may differ in sign. For instance, education may increase the *probability* of labour market participation insofar as it signifies higher skill levels and hence higher competitiveness, i.e. $\delta Prob(y_i > 0)/\delta Edu > 0$, where 'Edu' denotes education. But education may well have a negative effect on the *extent* of hiring-out if the relatively educated exhibit an aversion for manual labour (especially if done for others), i.e. $\delta E(y_i / y_i > 0)/\delta Edu < 0$. But this would be impossible in the tobit model where the probability of participation and the extent of participation are estimated jointly; for then both the effects are represented by one and the same coefficient (see Lin and Schmidt, 1984). For this reason, we prefer to estimate the labour supply models using the Heckman two-step procedure (Heckman, 1979). Note further, that not only does this procedure allow the signs of the coefficients to differ between the probit and regression models (comprising the tobit model), it also allows the set of regressors in the probit model to differ from that in the regression model. Although, in our case we do not find sufficient reason to hypothesize different sets of regressors for the probit and regression stages of the estimation procedure. Finally, note that using the two-step Heckman estimation procedure is not synonymous with using the 'Heckman model' *per se*. Heckman (1979) used his two-step procedure with a model which hypothesized both the hours of work and the wage rate to be jointly endogenous. As we have already argued in chapter 3, we consider it preferable to treat the wage rate as exogenous to household decision-making. In the first step, therefore, we estimate a probit maximum likelihood model (where y = 1 for positive off-farm labour supply and y = 0 otherwise), which tells us how the probability or likelihood of labour force participation by the household members is influenced by the various regressors. The estimation results are presented in Table 6.1 below. In the second step, we estimate a multiple regression of the extent of labour supply response, contingent on the participation decision in the first step. These results are reported in Table 6.2.

Before we proceed with the discussion of the results, let us briefly consider another important aspect of the estimation technique. Since we have cross section-time series (indeed, panel) data, an important question is how to pool these data. An acceptable mode of pooling the observations would be to include separate intercept terms for the cross-section units, for these provide natural sample partitions for parameter estimation. We feel,

Table 6.1 Total household labour supply by cultivator households: probit equation results

Dependent variable: Probability of desired off-Farm labour supply

Variable	Expected sign	Estimated coefficient	Asymptotic t-value
ERWR	+	0.176	0.378
ROP	+	0.772	0.972
AGE	?	−0.032	−2.455
EDU	?	−0.235	−5.787
CASTE	?	0.046	0.868
FS	+	0.035	0.590
PAM	?	0.350	2.518
PAF	?	−0.096	−0.837
EDM	?	0.302	1.274
EDF	?	0.481	1.690
GCA	−	−0.036	−3.644
PAIRR	−	−0.021	−3.465
INEXP	−	−0.00005	−1.151
NLASS	−	−0.00001	−0.635
CVNR	?	0.001	0.203
D1	?	1.399	2.139
D2	?	3.046	3.768
D3	?	2.561	3.803

Number of observations = 477
LR statistic (all slope coefficients = 0) = 261.02
Maddala R^2 = 0.4625
Cragg-Uhler R^2 = 0.6522
McFadden R^2 = 0.5026
Chow R^2 = 0.5559
Percentage of right predictions = 0.874

however, that pooling at the village level rather than the household level is sufficient in our case, for households residing within the geographical confines of a village may be expected to manifest similar behaviour as their environment is likely to be roughly homogeneous. Between villages, however, the differences may be expected to be large, especially if these villages are located far apart from each other, as the villages in our sample are (see also chapter 3). Assuming the regression coefficients to be fixed parameters, the above hypothesis would amount to using a separate intercept term for each village. Such a model was specified in the previous chapter in the context of the demand for labour and need not be repeated here (see equation 5.1). This may be a doubly preferable way of pooling the data, considering that our time series on individual households is too small (only nine observations), relative to the number of regressors that must be considered.[1]

Cultivator Households: Total Household Labour

Probit equation From the results in Table 6.1 we find that the likelihood of off-farm labour supply is positively but insignificantly related to the real wage rate. Similarly, the real price of the agricultural staple is positively but insignificantly related to the likelihood of labour force participation.[2] The respondents' age has a significantly negative effect on the probability of hiring-out. The number of years of education is negatively and highly significantly related to the regressand, this result being at variance with those of some of the earlier studies (see Sumner, 1982, and Huffman, 1980). It seems that education serves to improve the farmers' entrepreneurial ability, which gets reflected in a higher on-farm marginal product. This reduces the probability of his off-farm participation. Of course, implicit in this explanation is the hypothesis that entrepreneurial ability is not fully marketable. Further, this result may also be explained in terms of an aversion on the part of the educated in India (and other developing societies?) to do manual work, especially for others. It appears that a relatively higher position in the caste hierarchy would increase the probability of off-farm labour supply, but this effect is not statistically strong. The availability of prime age males and presence of elderly females increases the likelihood of wage labour supply. The latter effect is probably reflective of the fact that the presence of elderly females frees the younger lot from household chores, who can then supply their labour on the market. A larger gross cropped area and a larger percentage area irrigated both have a significant negative effect on the probability of wage labour participation. But while total input expenditure and nonland assets both have the expected negative sign they are not significant. Finally, nor is the production risk variable a significant determinant of the probability of hiring-out. The hypothesis that the regressors are all zero is strongly rejected at the 1%

Table 6.2 Total household labour supply by cultivator households: multiple regression adjusting for sample selection

Dependent variable: Desired off-Farm labour days

Variable	Expected sign	Estimated coefficient	T-value 311 d.o.f	Elasticity at means
ERWR	?	85.828	1.676	0.36
ROP	?	-82.248	-0.719	-0.23
AGE	?	1.058	0.514	0.23
EDU	?	-6.238	-0.673	-0.04
CASTE	?	-11.894	-1.601	-0.16
FS	+	-0.674	-0.083	-0.02
PAM	?	2.446	0.118	0.02
PAF	?	39.042	2.022	0.32
EDM	?	-44.529	-1.229	-0.07
EDF	?	44.432	1.056	0.06
GCA	-	-1.168	-0.717	-0.07
PAIRR	-	0.165	0.158	0.01
INEXP	-	-0.012	-2.073	-0.08
NLASS	-	-0.005	-2.354	-0.20
CVNR	?	-1.256	-2.259	-0.001
LAMBDA	?	6.018	0.069	0.01
D1	?	237.260	2.412	0.26
D2	?	138.820	1.294	0.19
D3	?	215.060	2.374	0.41

Number of observations = 330
LR statistic (all slope coefficients = 0) = 40.72
$\bar{R}^2$ = 0.1279

level, the *LR* statistic = 256.72 exceeding the critical value χ^2 (16 d.o.f) = 32.00. The percentage of correct predictions (of the binary dependent variable) using the probit model estimated is more than 87%.[3]

Multiple regression We now discuss the results in Table 6.2 pertaining to the off-farm labour supply response after adjusting for sample selection by the households in question. The hypothesis that all the regressors are jointly zero is rejected at the 1% level, the *LR* statistic = 35.48 exceeding the critical value χ^2 (16 d.o.f) = 32.00. Off-farm labour supply is found to be *positively* and significantly related to the real wage rate, with a reasonably large associated elasticity of 0.36. This result is in contrast to both Rosenzweig (1980) and Bardhan (1979a) who reported a *significantly negative* wage response for rural (male) labour in different samples of cultivator households in India. Although their findings may have been differed from ours on account of model mis-specification (specifically the omission of the risk variables), it is not quite possible to test this conjecture because the set of regressors, the definitions of the regressors and regressand, as well as the estimation methods differ between our three studies. But even so, it is indicative that when we estimate our model *excluding* the risk terms and define the regressand as *actual* rather than desired labour supply (so that the pertinent wage variable is the real wage rate rather than the expected real wage rate), we find that the labour supply response to the wage variable becomes significantly negative (Table 6.3). This should warn us of the importance of the correct specification.

Continuing with our discussion of the results in Table 6.2, the real price of the agricultural staple, ceteris paribus, is negatively insignificantly related to off-farm labour supply. Similarly, the age and education variables are also insignificant in explaining the extent of hiring-out. Interestingly, the number of prime age females in the family has a significant positive effect on hiring out. This is very much consistent with the observation of Walker and Ryan (1990), that in our sample villages the male members preferred to work on their own farms whereas female labour was supplied in the market. Therefore, the larger the number of prime age females in the family, ceteris paribus, the larger the supply of off-farm labour by the household. Total input expenditure and nonland assets both exert a significant negative effect on hiring-out. The larger the nonland assets and the greater the use of modern inputs such as high-yielding seeds and fertilisers, the larger would be the requirement of labour for self-cultivation. Consequently, the smaller would be the off-farm labour supply.

The multiplicative risk specification extends the farm household model by incorporating the moments of the revenue risk distribution. The coefficient of variation of net revenue turns out to be a highly significant determinant of the magnitude of labour force participation. Further, a likelihood ratio test for the nested models, i.e. the hypothesis that the true model does not include the production risk variable, supports the multiplicative risk specification at the 5% level, insofar as the *LR* test statistic (= 5.42) exceeds the critical value of χ^2 (1 d.o.f) (= 3.842). The

Table 6.3 Total household labour supply by cultivator households: multiple regression adjusting for sample selection

Dependent variable: Actual off-farm labour days

Variable	Expected sign	Estimated coefficient	T-value 307 d.o.f	Elasticity at means
RWR	?	-91.977	-2.589	-0.91
ROP	?	354.460	4.146	1.41
AGE	?	-1.566	-0.925	-0.48
EDU	?	-17.316	-2.287	-0.14
CASTE	?	-22.834	-3.906	-0.43
FS	+	-11.583	-1.728	-0.49
PAM	?	38.118	2.312	0.44
PAF	?	49.533	2.990	0.57
EDM	?	-8.175	-0.275	-0.02
EDF	?	94.869	2.760	0.16
GCA	–	-3.334	-2.540	-0.26
PAIRR	–	-0.912	-1.085	-0.04
INEXP	–	-0.011	-2.245	-0.10
NLASS	–	-0.001	-0.613	-0.07
LAMBDA	?	43.958	0.535	0.07
D1	?	164.270	1.925	0.25
D2	?	245.890	2.829	0.48
D3	?	206.490	2.666	0.56

Number of observations = 325
LR statistic (all slope coefficients = 0) = 60.40
$\bar{R}^2$ = 0.1335

significantly *negative* effect of the risk variable may seem somewhat counter-intuitive at first glance. For one may argue that as production risk increases, the farmer should move (his household labour) out of production into alternative activities, in this case the casual labour market. But note that in the rural setting centred around less developed agriculture, the employment option need not be any more viable. As we argued in chapter 4, production risk (weather shocks, for instance) may tend to carry forward into the local wage labour market and detrimentally affect the employment opportunities available there. This follows from the observation that weather shocks are not farm-specific but are likely to affect all the farms in a (small) given region, albeit to different extends. Therefore, insofar as an increase in the coefficient of variation of net returns also entails a tightening of the labour market, the magnitude of off-farm labour supply will decline.

It needs to be clarified that the above hypothesis about the increase in production risk leading to a tightening of the labour market is not necessarily contradictory to our finding in chapter 4 (of a statistically insignificant relationship between production risk and labour market risk). For statistical insignificance does not imply the lack of a relationship altogether. It merely implies that that relationship is not 'strong enough' to satisfy some predetermined, but nevertheless arbitrary, criterion. In other words, the relationship between production risk and labour market risk, although *technically* insignificant, may yet have been strong enough to result in the negative relationship between hiring-out and production risk. Thus, our result may be taken to imply that higher production uncertainty may not only reduce the cultivator households' income from on-farm production but may also possibly reduce their income from off-farm employment.

Cultivator Households: Female Labour

Interest in the issue of the off-farm labour supply of women has been more than a matter of mere detail. A host of reasons have contributed to focus attention on this particular sub-group within the household. While the contribution of women within the household has never been doubted, their respect in society has tended to be coloured, *inter alia*, by their income earning ability. Second, even when family prestige has been equated with womenfolk *not* working outside the household, sheer economic necessity often drives them into the labour market. This would be especially true in the rural developing country context. Third, during certain stages in the agricultural cycle, such as sowing and harvest times, there is often additional demand for prompt and efficient labour. At such times the slack in the male labour market often vanishes and female labour supply assumes more importance. In this context, it would be of interest to know whether, and to what extent, female labour supply responds to economic incentives. Finally, of course, given that the female participation rate *has* increased over time, it is of interest to know whether women as a group respond any differently from men.

In this section we look into the influence of various economic, social and demographic factors on the wage labour response of females from cultivator households. We begin with a discussion of the modifications that need to be made to the economic model in view of the fact that we are focusing on a particular sub-group within the household. It is often argued, that traditionally female participation in the work force has been treated as a supplementary source of income, the primary source being the male members of the family. Given this situation, the real expected wage rate for males (ERWRM) becomes a pertinent determinant of female wage labour supply. For if the male wage rate (and, therefore, the family income) were to go up sufficiently, the family may consider it unnecessary for the females in the household to supply the current amount of market labour (or to supply any market labour at all). Holding the female workers' ages constant, an increase in the age of the male working members (AGEM) would increase the probability of female labour force participation. Lastly, assuming the education of the male workers in the household to be complementary to that of the female workers, we would expect female wage labour to be negatively related to the education of the male members in the family (EDUM).

For the estimation exercises in this section, the 'basic' sample of 53 households (see chapter 3) was pruned to remove the female-headed households. This left us with 51 households or 510 observations to begin with. The probit estimation results relating to the probability of female labour force participation are given in Table 6.4, while Table 6.5 reports the results for the magnitude of female off-farm labour supply response.[4]

Probit equation Table 6.4 tells us that the expected real wage rates for females and males are both insignificant in determining the likelihood of labour market participation by the females in the farm household. A higher age of the female workers significantly increases the likelihood of labour supply, perhaps because it implies greater experience. One wonders if this positive 'age effect' also reflects a sociological aspect — namely, that older women are relatively independent (of the male household head's authority) and this gets reflected in a higher likelihood of labour force participation. Of the household composition variables, a larger number of elderly dependent males reduce the likelihood of participation. A larger gross cropped area and higher nonland assets strongly reduce the probability of hiring-out female labour. The production risk variable exercises a significant, positive influence on the probability of female off-farm labour supply. Since male labour is preferred for self-cultivation, when the risk

Table 6.4 Female labour supply by cultivator households: probit equation results

Dependent variable: Probability of desired off-Farm labour days

Variable	Expected sign	Estimated coefficient	Asymptotic t-value
ERWRF	+	−0.010	−0.013
ERWRM	−	0.228	0.679
ROP	+	0.144	0.206
AGEF	?	0.022	2.451
AGEM	?	0.003	0.264
EDUF	?	−0.014	−0.243
EDUM	?	−0.053	−1.307
CASTE	?	0.064	1.467
FS	+	0.077	1.584
PAM	?	−0.052	−0.476
PAF	?	0.084	0.752
EDM	?	−0.408	−2.235
EDF	?	−0.293	−1.433
GCA	−	−0.019	−2.266
PAIRR	−	0.0004	0.080
INEXP	−	−0.00005	−1.230
NLASS	−	−0.00007	−4.661
CVNR	?	0.049	1.676
D1	?	−0.321	−0.590
D2	?	−0.588	−0.834
D3	?	−0.483	−0.739

Number of observations = 459
LR statistic (all slope coefficients = 0) = 214.94
Maddala R^2 = 0.3779
Cragg-Uhler R^2 = 0.5040
McFadden R^2 = 0.3426
Chow R^2 = 0.4285
Percentage of right predictions = 0.786

associated with self-cultivation increases the probability of female labour

Table 6.5 Female labour supply by cultivator households: multiple regression adjusting for sample selection

Dependent variable: Desired off-Farm labour days

Variable	Expected sign	Estimated coefficient	T-value 214 d.o.f	Elasticity at means
ERWRF	?	−29.127	−0.294	−0.09
ERWRM	?	13.538	0.295	0.10
ROP	?	16.636	0.169	0.07
AGEF	?	−6.581	−3.886	−1.51
AGEM	?	1.526	1.221	0.51
EDUF	?	−10.194	−1.223	−0.05
EDUM	?	12.063	1.742	0.09
CASTE	?	−12.374	−1.804	−0.27
FS	+	−1.063	−0.153	−0.05
PAM	?	−8.341	−0.593	−0.10
PAF	?	−19.548	−0.987	−0.23
EDM	?	3.386	0.083	0.01
EDF	?	63.281	1.960	0.11
GCA	−	−1.406	−0.775	−0.09
PAIRR	−	−0.615	−0.866	−0.03
INEXP	−	−0.008	−1.299	−0.07
NLASS	−	0.021	3.377	0.91
CVNR	?	−3.765	−1.672	−0.03
LAMBDA	?	−268.740	−2.530	−0.89
D1	?	376.920	3.027	0.90
D2	?	365.520	2.412	0.49
D3	?	416.110	2.881	1.21

Number of observations = 236
LR statistic (all slope coefficients = 0) = 39.40
R^2 = 0.1474

being shifted into employment in the casual labour market goes up. The estimated model correctly predicts about 79% of the observations, and a likelihood ratio test strongly rejects the hypothesis that the regressors are all zero.

Table 6.6   Total household labour supply by landless households: probit equation results

Dependent variable: Probability of desired labour days supplied

Variable	Expected sign	Estimated coefficient	Asymptotic t-value
ERWR	+	2.621	1.660
AGE	?	-0.063	-0.601
EDU	?	-0.713	-1.267
CASTE	?	0.217	0.372
FS	+	1.258	1.310
PAM	?	0.596	0.591
PAF	?	-1.010	-0.786
EDM	?	-1.508	-0.439
EDF	?	-0.603	-0.393
NLASS	–	-0.001	-2.280
AVCVNR	?	0.374	1.718
D1	?	1.097	0.203
D2	?	4.410	0.660
D3	?	2.896	0.626

Number of observations = 207
LR statistic (all slope coefficients = 0) = 33.23
Maddala R^2 = 0.1547
Cragg-Uhler R^2 = 0.6046
McFadden R^2 = 0.5687
Chow R^2 = 0.3965
Percentage of right predictions = 0.966

Multiple regression Coming to the results of the second step of the Heckman procedure (Table 6.5), we find that the real expected female and male wage rates are insignificant determinants of the *amount* of female off-farm labour supply. A higher female age reduces the amount of labour supplied off-farm, signifying the debilitating effects of age. Higher male education increases the female off-farm labour supply. Caste appears to have a significant negative effect on the extent of hiring-out, supporting the hypothesis about family prestige attached to females *not* working off the farm. A higher number of dependent females facilitates hiring out by the working age females. Production risk significantly negatively influences the magnitude of female labour supply. Even though a higher coefficient of variation leads to an increase in the probability of hiring-out as we saw above, that does not mean that the actual labour sold on the market goes up. As we had argued earlier, if increasing production risk decreases the labour market opportunities, actual labour supply may decline. The sample selection bias variable is highly significant. Although a likelihood ratio test does not support the inclusion of the risk variables in the model, the hypothesis that the regressors are all zero is strongly rejected.

Landless Households: Total Household Labour

This group of labour suppliers is, by definition, very different from the cultivator households. We have already discussed these differences in chapters 2 and 3. In this section we analyse the factors that determine their labour supply behaviour. The probit function estimates are given in Table 6.6, while Table 6.7 presents the estimation results of the magnitude of labour supply after adjusting for sample selection.

Probit equation From Table 6.6 we find that the probability of labour market participation is positively significantly related to the expected real wage rate. The availability of nonland assets has a strong negative influence on the likelihood of labour market participation. Nonland assets in this case do not refer to farm buildings, cultivation implements and machinery etc, since the landless do not cultivate by definition. They refer, instead, to livestock, and more work in animal husbandry would decrease the probability of hiring-out. The production risk variable, which influences the opportunities in the labour market, is significantly positive. This appears somewhat inexplicable but perhaps isn't. For worsening labour market conditions on account of an increase in production risk may depress the *actual* days worked, but by increasing the involuntary unemployment by a greater proportion may result in an increase in the likelihood of *desired* labour supply. The estimated model predicts about 97% of the observations correctly, and a likelihood ratio test strongly rejects the hypothesis that the slope coefficients are all zero.

Multiple regression Given the decision to participate in the labour market, we find that caste status strongly and positively affects the extent of hiring-out (Table 6.7). The remaining results are generally poor, as was true of

Table 6.7 Total household labour supply by landless households: multiple regression adjusting for sample selection

Dependent variable: Desired labour days supplied

Variable	Expected sign	Estimated coefficient	T-value 185 d.o.f	Elasticity at means
ERWR	?	−43.436	−0.595	−0.12
AGE	?	0.127	0.053	0.02
EDU	?	−11.915	−0.958	−0.02
CASTE	?	35.146	3.054	0.50
FS	+	1.320	0.088	0.02
PAM	?	−43.512	−1.624	−0.21
PAF	?	61.026	1.897	0.23
EDM	?	25.037	0.463	0.02
EDF	?	55.330	1.220	0.04
NLASS	−	0.039	2.342	0.33
AVCVNR	?	−3.867	−0.553	−0.001
LAMBDA	?	−102.940	−0.735	−0.01
D1	?	−62.062	−0.409	−0.07
D2	?	60.844	0.426	0.08
D3	?	224.400	1.854	0.19

Number of observations = 200
LR statistic (all slope coefficients = 0) = 24.42
$\bar{R}^2$ = 0.1394

Rosenzweig (1980) for another sample of landless households, although a likelihood ratio test rejects the null hypothesis that the regressors are all zero.

Wage Functions

The extant literature presents a host of theories of rural wage determination. While a critical review of the alternative theories is beyond the scope of the present undertaking, some comments are in order. Two classes of theories appear to be irrelevant in our specific context, which is wage determination

Table 6.8 Wage function for total household labour supply by cultivator households

Variable	Estimated coefficient	T-value 460 d.o.f	Elasticity at means
ROP	2.463	8.399	0.37
AGE	-0.013	-1.357	-0.16
EDU	-0.050	-1.931	-0.03
CASTE	-0.133	-3.247	-0.09
FS	-0.137	-2.898	-0.23
PAM	0.440	4.542	0.20
PAF	0.161	1.580	0.07
EDM	0.344	1.796	0.03
EDF	0.453	2.180	0.03
GCA	-0.012	-1.816	-0.05
PAIRR	-0.004	-0.833	-0.01
INEXP	-0.000003	-0.104	-0.001
NLASS	0.00004	5.393	0.14
CVNR	0.003	0.814	0.00
D1	1.950	3.481	0.16
D2	4.529	8.393	0.26
D3	3.223	6.334	0.31

Number of observations = 477
LR statistic (all slope coefficients = 0) = 171.74
$\bar{R}^2$ = 0.4237

in *daily* casual labour markets. These are the efficiency wage theories and those involving implicit contracts. For almost by definition these theories relate to longer time periods, certainly longer than a single day (Rosenzweig, 1988). A third theory, that of interlinked markets, is not consistent with our sample, since interlinked transactions were mostly limited to 'regular farm servants' or tied labour in these villages (Jodha, 1984; Binswanger *et.al.*, 1984; Walker and Ryan, 1990). A fourth class of theories, the so-called subsistence theories, is not supported by the econometric evidence that we present below. This class of theories hypothesizes that real wages are determined for the most part by factors that are exogenous to the labour market, such as cultural/social, biological

Table 6.9 Wage function for female labour supply by cultivator households

Variable	Estimated coefficient	T-value 442 d.o.f	Elasticity at means
ROP	2.251	8.651	0.48
AGE	−0.006	−0.775	−0.06
EDU	−0.052	−1.332	−0.03
CASTE	−0.052	−1.430	−0.05
FS	−0.122	−3.024	−0.28
PAM	0.135	1.578	0.08
PAF	0.276	3.038	0.18
EDM	0.026	0.182	0.003
EDF	0.129	0.761	0.01
GCA	0.002	0.410	0.01
PAIRR	−0.004	−0.969	−0.01
INEXP	0.00002	0.771	0.01
NLASS	0.00001	1.291	0.04
CVNR	0.002	0.529	0.00
D1	1.499	4.187	0.18
D2	2.608	6.810	0.20
D3	1.731	4.842	0.24

Number of observations = 459
LR statistic (all slope coefficients = 0) = 113.62
$\bar{R}^2$ = 0.2557

or moral norms. In other words, these theories may be interpreted to predict that changes in labour market conditions have no effect on wage rates. The evidence provided below, however, does not support this assertion.

Wage Function for Cultivator Households

We first analyse the wage function pertaining to the total household labour supply of cultivator households (Table 6.8). The regressors include various personal and household characteristic variables, as well as demand-side and productivity variables. An increase in the real price of the agricultural staple has a very significant positive effect on the daily wage rate, with an

Table 6.10 Wage function for male labour supply by cultivator households

Variable	Estimated coefficient	T-value 442 d.o.f	Elasticity at means
ROP	-0.265	-0.209	-0.03
AGE	0.009	0.251	0.07
EDU	-0.026	-0.228	-0.01
CASTE	0.024	0.136	0.01
FS	-0.224	-1.141	-0.23
PAM	0.603	1.441	0.17
PAF	0.220	0.504	0.06
EDM	-0.082	-0.111	-0.004
EDF	0.201	0.239	0.01
GCA	-0.011	-0.403	-0.03
PAIRR	-0.0002	-0.011	0.00
INEXP	0.0003	1.898	0.07
NLASS	0.00003	0.737	0.05
CVNR	0.004	0.249	0.00
D1	4.024	1.846	0.22
D2	5.078	2.356	0.18
D3	7.447	3.650	0.47

Number of observations = 459
LR statistic (all slope coefficients = 0) = 8.38
R^2 = 0.0301

associated elasticity of 0.37. An increase in the price of the agricultural staple leads to an induced demand for labour which exerts an upward pressure on the wage rate. The education level has a negative coefficient, which seems counter-intuitive; for even if the relatively educated do not receive a premium wage why should they get a relatively lower wage? Of the adults and children contributing to household labour supply, children are probably relatively more educated since formal education has picked up only in the recent past. Since their wages are lower than those of adults, this might make for a negative relation between education and the wage rate (of children). But for total labour supply this explanation is incomplete since child labour comprises a very small proportion of the total household labour. Caste status also has a negative and significant effect on the wage rate. Again, this appears somewhat counter-intuitive. A possible explanation could be that high caste workers are neither willing to work for lower caste households nor in certain relatively menial operations. Consequently, they may be willing to work at lower wage rates as a price for working for preferred employers/operations. There appears to be some evidence that the more the dependents (females and males) in the family, the higher the wage rate. Perhaps families with relatively less dependents are willing to work at somewhat lower wages, but those with more dependents cannot 'afford' to. Larger nonland assets, by increasing the demand for hired labour, lead to higher wage rates.

Wage Functions for Cultivator Households: Female and Male Labour

Within the group of cultivator households, it is of interest to see whether the wage functions of male and female labour are any different from each other, and from that for household labour as a whole. From Table 6.9 we find that the wage function results for female labour are almost the same as those discussed above for total labour supply with regard to coefficient signs. The difference is in the changed significance of some variables — the counter-intuitively negative education and caste variables are no longer significant. In the case of the wage function for male labour (Table 6.10), the only slope variable that turns out to be significant is total input expenditure. An increase in such expenditure, by inducing an increased use of labour in self-cultivation, would lead to a decrease in market labour supply and hence result in higher wage rates.

Wage Function for Landless Households

For the group of landless households, Table 6.11 reveals that a larger family size is associated with a lower wage rate. A larger supply of labour to the market on account of larger household sizes would lead to a downward pressure on the wage rate. Larger nonland assets (livestock, for example), by absorbing more labour in animal husbandry, decreases wage labour supply, which exerts an upward pressure on the wage rate. An increase in the average coefficient of variation of net revenue (AVCVNR) is negatively related to the wage rate. Thus, worsening labour market opportunities (on account of an increase in production risk) would depress the wage rate.

Gathering the above wage function results together, we are led to the

**Table 6.11 Wage function for total household labour supply by
landless households**

Variable	Estimated coefficient	T-value 194 d.o.f	Elasticity at means
AGE	0.004	0.271	0.05
EDU	0.109	1.392	0.02
CASTE	0.045	0.736	0.05
FS	-0.190	-2.318	-0.24
PAM	-0.068	-0.415	-0.02
PAF	0.360	2.105	0.11
EDM	0.032	0.096	0.003
EDF	0.103	0.376	0.01
NLASS	0.0003	5.265	0.22
AVCVNR	-0.060	-1.776	-0.01
D1	2.598	2.809	0.23
D2	3.691	4.262	0.37
D3	3.388	4.571	0.22

Number of observations = 207
LR statistic (all slope coefficients = 0) = 50.55
$\bar{R}^2$ = 0.2861

conclusion that the process of wage determination in the daily casual labour
markets in these regions is inconsistent with the subsistence theories. Our
results show that wage rates are significantly responsive to demand side
variables, human capital variables, and family size and composition
variables.

A Disequilibrium Model of the Labour Market

While studies considering casual labour supply *in insolation* are certainly
useful, they may provide unreliable parameter estimates since the demand
for labour is often the 'shorter side' of rural labour markets in developing
agriculture. Similarly, while estimating the demand for labour *alone* may
prove useful, during periods of intense activity such as sowing and
harvesting there is often excess demand for labour and labour supply

becomes the shorter side of the market. Therefore, better estimates of the labour supply and labour demand parameters may be obtainable if we could estimate the labour supply and labour demand functions simultaneously. Keeping this objective in mind, let the aggregate off-farm labour supply function be specified as:

$$L^s = X_1 \beta_1 + \epsilon_1$$

where L^s is actual labour supply, X_1 is the vector of explanatory variables including the real wage rate (RWR), β_1 is the parameter vector and ϵ_1 is the error term. Similarly, the aggregate demand for labour function may be specified as

$$L^d = X_2 \beta_2 + \epsilon_2$$

where L^d is labour demand, X_2 is the vector of explanatory variables including the real wage rate, β_2 is the parameter vector and ϵ_2 is the error term.

In solving this simultaneous equations model it would be inappropriate to assume that the labour market is in equilibrium (as does Bardhan, 1984b). For a stylized fact of rural labour markets in developing Asian agriculture is that they do not clear. While they are mostly characterized by excess supply, there are short periods during sowing and harvest times when they exhibit excess demand. This is usually modelled by assuming that the amount of labour transacted is determined by the shorter side of the market, i.e. $L = min\ (L^s,\ L^d)$. Following Fair and Jaffee (1972), we hypothesize that the change in the real wage rate is a positive function of the difference between the demand and supply of labour, i.e. $\Delta RWR = \lambda(L^d - L^s)$, $\lambda > 0$. Further, the speed of adjustment of the wage rate may vary depending on whether wages are rising or falling. Thus $\Delta RWR = \lambda_1(L^d - L^s)$ when $L^d < L^s$, and $\Delta RWR = \lambda_2(L^d - L^s)$ when $L^d > L^s$ (Laffont and Garcia, 1977).

In employing this model we face a problem. As we have already seen, the supply of labour emanates from two distinct groups — cultivator households and landless households. Since cultivator households are both consumers and producers of their staples, their supply of labour (or consumption of leisure) is likely to be influenced by various production side variables as well. This would not be true of landless households, who are not producers by definition. Therefore, these two groups are characterised by distinct labour supply functions. Although our data set provides labour supply figures by source, i.e. the supply that emanates from the cultivator households and that which comes from the landless households, data on the demand for labour is available only in the aggregate. In other words when we consider the demand for labour, we have no way of knowing what part of it arises from cultivator households and what part from the landless households. Consequently, we cannot conduct simultaneous equations analyses for cultivator households and landless households separately. But perhaps nor would this be desirable, considering that both sets of households operate in the *same* casual labour market. Therefore, we proceed as follows. Let the aggregate off-farm labour supply functions of these two household groups be:

$$L^{s1} = X_1^1 \, \beta_1^1 + \epsilon_1^1$$

$$L^{s2} = X_1^2 \, \beta_1^2 + \epsilon_1^2$$

such that

$$L^s = L^{s1} + L^{s2}$$

where L^{s1} is the aggregate off-farm labour supply of cultivator households, L^{s2} is the aggregate off-farm labour supply of landless households, and L^s is total off-farm labour supply. Our complete model is then given by the following set of equations:

$$L^{s1} = X_1^1 \, \beta_1^1 + \epsilon_1^1$$

$$L^{s2} = X_1^2 \, \beta_1^2 + \epsilon_1^2$$

$$L^s = L^{s1} + L^{s2}$$

$$L^d = X_2\beta_2 + \epsilon_2$$

$$L = \min(L^s, L^d)$$

$$\Delta RWR = \lambda_1(L^d - L^s) \text{ when } L^d < L^s$$

$$\Delta RWR = \lambda_2(L^d - L^s) \text{ when } L^d > L^s \tag{6.1a)-(6.1g)}$$

Note, that in this system of equations we consider the actual and not the desired supply of labour (and, correspondingly, the actual not the expected real wage rate), since we have explicitly allowed for the labour market disequilibrium, and hence do not need to include the involuntary unemployment in the labour supply variable. Further, the real wage rate is also an exogenous variable. Using changes in this variable as the 'sample separator', for $\Delta RWR > 0$ we have $L^d > L^s$, so that $L = L^s$ or

$$L = X_1^1 \beta_1^1 + X_1^2 \beta_1^2 + \epsilon_1^1 + \epsilon_1^2 \qquad (6.2)$$

Also, from system (6.1), $L = L^d - (1/\lambda_2)\Delta RWR$, which implies that

$$L = X_2\beta_2 + \epsilon_2 - (1/\lambda_2)\Delta RWR \qquad (6.3)$$

Similarly, for $\Delta RWR < 0$ we have $L^d < L^s$, so that $L = L^d$ or

$$L = X_2\beta_2 + \epsilon_2 \qquad (6.4)$$

Again, from system (6.1), $L = L^s + (1/\lambda_1)\Delta RWR$, which implies that

$$L = X_1^1 \beta_1^1 + X_1^2 \beta_1^2 + \epsilon_1^1 + \epsilon_1^2 + (1/\lambda_1)\Delta RWR \qquad (6.5)$$

From (6.2) and (6.5) we get the off-farm labour supply functions of cultivator and landless households as, respectively:

$$L^{s1} = X_1^1 \beta_1^1 + (1/\lambda_1)h_1 + \epsilon_1^1 \qquad (6.6)$$

$$L^{s2} = X_1^2 \beta_1^2 + (1/\lambda_1)h_1 + \epsilon_1^2 \qquad (6.7)$$

where $h_1 = \Delta RWR$ for $\Delta RWR \leq 0$, and 0 otherwise. From (6.3) and (6.4) we get the demand function for labour as:

$$L = X_2\beta_2 - 1/\lambda_2 \, h_2 + \epsilon_2 \qquad (6.8)$$

where $h_2 = \Delta RWR$ for $\Delta RWR \geq 0$, and 0 otherwise.

Consistent estimates of the supply and demand parameters may be obtained using Amemiya's two-step procedure (Amemiya, 1974). In the first step, regress the variables RWR, h_1 and h_2 on all the exogenous variables using all the observations. In the second step, using these instrumental variables, estimate equations (6.6), (6.7) and (6.8) by ordinary least squares to derive 2SLS estimates. Ideally, equations (6.6) and (6.7)

Table 6.12 Aggregate off-farm labour supply by cultivator households: disequilibrium model, GLS estimates

Dependent variable: Aggregate desired off-Farm labour days

Variable	Regression coefficient	Asymptotic t-value	Elasticity at means
RWR	915.91	0.867	0.89
ROP	-3378.30	-1.344	-1.60
AGE	375.49	2.760	13.96
EDU	-150.43	-0.177	-0.28
CASTE	-250.61	-0.534	-0.55
FS	738.92	1.195	3.82
PAM	-2506.20	-1.563	-3.53
PAF	904.30	0.548	1.30
EDM	-3937.60	-0.966	-1.08
EDF	234.46	0.090	0.05
GCA	131.60	1.340	1.66
PAIRR	49.19	0.965	0.49
INEXP	-0.47	-2.142	-0.55
NLASS	0.23	3.962	1.97
CVNR	134.26	1.825	0.05
H1	-6361.20	-2.139	0.05
D1	-22497.00	-2.755	-5.56
D2	-22031.00	-2.657	-5.44
D3	-18785.00	-2.096	-4.64

$R^2 = 0.8921$

Number of observations = 27

Wald statistic (all slopes = 0) = 139.37, with p-value = 0.000

should be estimated under the restriction that the coefficient of regressor h_1 be the same in both equations. Not observing this restriction, however, would only result in some loss in efficiency; the consistency of the estimators would remain unaltered. Relatively efficient estimates may be obtained by generalised least squares, by estimating the equations jointly. Statistical significance of variable h_1 would signal the presence of equilibrium or excess supply in the casual labour market over the sample period, whereas significance of variable h_2 would signal equilibrium or excess demand. Furthermore, if the estimate of $1/\lambda_1$ exceeds the estimate of $1/\lambda_2$ that would imply wage stickiness in the downward direction.

Estimation Results from the Disequilibrium Model

In order to estimate the equations derived above, we must first decide upon what constitutes the 'market' in which the supply and demand for labour interact. As we pointed out in chapter 4, surveying a large number of studies on rural labour markets in different parts of India, Dreze and Mukherjee (1989) observe that '[T]he village labour market is largely *closed*: labour hiring across neighbouring villages is rare' (italics in the original). Thus, it appears that the village would be the appropriate unit for studying the demand-supply interactions in the Indian casual labour markets. Therefore, we derive the aggregate off-farm labour supplied and demanded by aggregating across all the households in a given village in a given year. As for the regressors, the village-level real wage rate is derived as a weighted average of the wage rates received by labour from the cultivator and landless households, using the relative shares of these households in the total off-farm labour supplied as weights. The other village-level exogenous variables were derived as simple averages across all the households in a given village in a given year. In the demand for hired labour equation (6.8), these other regressors comprise the real output price, age of the household head, education of the household head, caste, family size, prime age males, prime age females, elderly dependent males, elderly dependent females, gross cropped area, percentage area irrigated, input expenditure, nonland assets, coefficient of variation of net revenue, and village dummies. In labour supply equation (6.6) for cultivator households, the regressors include the same set of variables as above. In supply equation (6.7) for landless households, the set of regressors does not contain the real output price, gross cropped area, percentage area irrigated, input expenditure and coefficient of variation of net revenue, for the obvious reason that landless households do not cultivate by definition. Additionally, the variables education and caste had to be dropped from equation (6.7) in order to prevent a positive definite design matrix.[5] Note that the village dummies serve the dual purpose of pooling the panel data by allowing for a different intercept for each of the cross section units, namely the villages. We estimate equations (6.6), (6.7) and (6.8) by generalised least squares, and the estimation results are reported in Tables 6.12 to 6.14.

Table 6.13 Aggregate labour supply by landless households: disequilibrium model, GLS estimates

Dependent variable: Aggregate desired off-Farm labour days

Variable	Regression coefficient	Asymptotic t-value	Elasticity at means
RWR	-476.32	-1.972	-0.57
AGE	477.45	4.336	22.33
FS	-412.89	-0.915	-1.87
PAM	-770.71	-0.721	-0.96
PAF	454.43	0.502	0.46
EDM	-264.14	-0.169	-0.08
EDF	749.47	0.380	0.16
NLASS	-0.55	-2.491	-1.34
H1	-6261.20	-2.139	0.06
D1	-20613.00	-3.571	-6.23
D2	-17998.00	-3.390	-5.44
D3	-18234.00	-3.567	-5.51

$\bar{R}^2 = 0.7484$
Number of observations = 27
Wald statistic (all slopes = 0) = 82.79, with p-value = 0.000

The estimation results are rather good. The hypothesis that the slope coefficients are all zero is strongly rejected for all three equations. Many of the explanatory variables are significant in the regressions. Regressors that have the wrong sign *and* turn out to be significant are the exception. Table 6.12 informs us that the aggregate off-farm labour supply from cultivator households is positively, albeit insignificantly, related to the real wage rate variable; the associated elasticity being 0.89. Although this may not be considered to contradict the results of Bardhan (1979) and Rosenzweig (1980) who reported a significantly negative wage response of (male) labour supply for Indian cultivator households, it does not lend support to their results either. Age is found to have a strong positive effect on hiring-out. Input expenditure in self-cultivation significantly reduces market labour supply. Nonland assets has an inexplicably positive sign; this being the only unexpected sign that is also significant. The production risk

Table 6.14   Aggregate demand for hired labour: disequilibrium model, GLS estimates

Dependent variable: Aggregate demand for hired labour days

Variable	Regression coefficient	Asymptotic t-value	Elasticity at means
RWR	−3978.30	−2.336	−1.29
ROP	7468.80	2.185	1.18
AGE	−28.80	−0.195	−0.36
EDU	−273.64	−0.194	−0.17
CASTE	−1284.90	−0.923	−0.94
FS	−867.87	−0.583	−1.49
PAM	−2398.40	−1.191	−1.12
PAF	131.46	0.049	0.06
EDM	−1648.20	−0.367	−0.15
EDF	165.55	0.058	0.01
GCA	38.14	0.256	0.16
PAIRR	−19.90	−0.347	−0.07
INEXP	0.92	1.696	0.36
NLASS	−0.39	−1.568	−1.12
CVNR	−333.26	−1.287	−0.04
H2	6468.50	0.891	0.21
D1	21863.00	1.051	1.79
D2	21541.00	0.941	1.77
D3	26831.00	1.036	2.20

$R^2 = 0.9538$
Number of observations = 27
Wald statistic (all slopes = 0) = 44.11, with p-value = 0.000

variable exercises a significant positive influence on off-farm labour supply. This would lend credence to the hypothesis that the cultivator households use the labour market as a hedge against production risk, moving out of self-cultivation and into the labour market.

From Table 6.13 we find that the aggregate labour supply from landless households is significantly negatively related to the real wage rate. This contradicts the results of Bardhan (*ibid.*) and Rosenzweig (*ibid.*), the

Table 6.15 Aggregate wage function

Dependent variable: (Weighted average) real wage rate

Variable	Regression coefficient	T-value 10 d.o.f	Elasticity at means
ROP	1.63	2.998	0.28
AGE	0.10	1.052	1.38
EDU	1.27	2.467	0.84
CASTE	0.19	0.577	0.15
FS	−0.33	−0.736	−0.60
PAM	−0.09	−0.077	−0.05
PAF	1.19	1.072	0.61
EDM	−1.80	−0.627	−0.18
EDF	2.24	1.243	0.16
GCA	−0.04	−0.733	−0.19
PAIRR	−0.01	−0.468	−0.05
INEXP	−0.00001	−0.074	−0.01
NLASS	0.0001	3.410	0.42
CVNR	0.003	0.064	0.001
D1	−7.23	−1.274	−0.64
D2	−5.25	−0.903	−0.46
D3	−7.59	−1.291	−0.67

$\bar{R}^2 = 0.9348$
Number of observations = 27
LR statistic (all slopes = 0) = 91.89

former reporting a significantly positive wage response for the landless and the latter an insignificant response. Bardhan (1984b) found labour supply to be significantly positively related to the wage rate, but this pertains to *total* labour supply, i.e. labour supply from cultivator plus landless households. Secondly, he estimated the simultaneous equations model under the assumption that the labour market clears, which is not tenable. Age has a highly significant positive effect on hiring-out. Higher nonland assets decrease hiring-out significantly.

Coming to the demand for hired labour, Table 6.14 reveals that the aggregate demand for hired labour is negatively significantly related to the real wage rate, with an associated elasticity of about -1.4. This is in agreement with the result of Evenson and Binswanger (1984), but contradicts that of Bardhan (1984b) who reports the wage variable to be insignificant in explaining hired labour demand. An increase in the real output price induces a strong increase in the demand for labour. Caste factors do not appear to determine the demand for labour. Input expenditure in self-cultivation reduces hiring-in, the associated elasticity being -0.36.

The sample separation variable h_2 in the demand equation has the right sign but turns out to be insignificant. On the other hand, variable h_1 in the supply equations also has the right sign and is highly significant. This implies that most of the sample period was characterised by excess supply or equilibrium in the casual labour market in our study regions. Furthermore, the null hypothesis that the estimate of $1/\lambda_1$ (the absolute value of the coefficient of h_1) does *not* exceed the estimate of $1/\lambda_2$ (the absolute value of the coefficient of h_2) is rejected, since the Wald statistic (1 d.o.f) is 2.195 which has a p-value of 0.138. Thus, the estimate of $1/\lambda_1$ significantly exceeds the estimate of $1/\lambda_2$, implying that the speed of wage adjustment in the upward direction exceeds that in the downward direction. These results are consistent with the stylized facts in Asian rural labour markets, characterised as they are by involuntary unemployment and wage-stickiness in the downward direction. Finally, from the wage function results in Table 6.15 we find that the (weighted average) real wage rate responds positively and significantly to the real output price, education and cultivators' nonland assets.

The disequilibrium model results discussed above are, however, subject to some caveats. Its computation requires village-level data, but aggregation of the household data across villages raises certain problems. First, it lessens the variation in the variables. While normally this need not prove a handicap, in the case of our data set there is rather little variation in some of the variables to begin with. As a result, aggregation just compounds the problem. Thus, the reason that the household size and composition variables are consistently insignificant in all the regressions is probably this lack of variation across the sample villages. Secondly, aggregation leaves us with nine observations over 1976-1984 for each of the three villages, or a total of only 27 observations. This sample size is rather small in view of the large number of regressors that we need to consider, and would lead to large sample variances of the parameter estimates. Therefore, although these simultaneous equations results generally support, indeed complement, those of the partial analyses of the casual labour market discussed earlier, we place greater confidence in the latter and prefer to retain the conclusions drawn from them.

Notes

1   Note that more complicated pooled models, such as the cross-sectionally heteroscedastic time-wise autoregressive model (Kmenta, 1986), are not available for censored variables; and certainly not as part of econometrics software. Also see chapter 5 on the drawbacks of this model.
2   When the alternative hypothesis is 'one-sided' (i.e. the expected sign of the coefficient in question is either positive or else negative) we use a one-tail test, but when it is 'two-sided' (i.e. the expected sign could be positive or negative) we use a two-tail test of significance.
3   An observation t is predicted to be $y_t = 1$ if the index or indicator variable I_t is positive or zero, otherwise the observation is predicted to be $y_t = 0$.
4   The empirical analysis presented in this section differs somewhat from that in Kanwar (1995), where only those households (out of the 'basic' 53) were retained which reported the presence of both the (male) household head as well as the spouse over the survey period. This resulted in a significantly smaller sample size. Moreover, the model specification here improves upon the earlier one by including in the set of regressors two other production side variables ('percentage area irrigated' and 'total input expenditure'), and also variables that capture the age and sex composition of the household members.
5   There was little variation in these two variables to begin with — the landless households are uniformly amongst the least educated, and belong to the lower castes (see chapter 3). And the process of averaging across the village households in order to construct the village-level variables reduced the variation even more. Together with the village dummies, this was resulting in the 'dummy variable trap'.

7 Summing Up

The Basic Method

This study is motivated by the fact that the overwhelming burden of previous empirical research into the issues of farmers' off-farm labour allocation, their hiring-in behaviour, the process of rural wage determination, and related matters, ignored the presence of risk as a variable of potential importance. We find this to be a potentially serious omission, given the nature of agricultural enterprise. An additional reason for the need to correct this error of omission stems from the undesirable statistical implications of an omitted variable mis-specification. Structural analyses ignoring the presence of risk, therefore, are likely to lead to incorrect estimating models and misleading inferences. Yet another reason for undertaking this study stems from our observation that the theoretical analyses of the individual consumer and the farm household under risk have had few unambiguous results to offer. Even on rather simple assumptions regarding the underlying framework employed, the theoretical results are found to depend crucially on the third derivative properties of the utility function and other limiting parameterisations, about which we have no strong priors. In the event, recourse to empirical estimation at some stage becomes unavoidable.

We model the farm household's decision-making process within the framework of a farm household model under production risk, wherein the household is assumed to maximise the expected utility of a static multi-argument utility function. Using this framework, it becomes evident that the conclusions from the model turn on the interplay between the risk attitudes and the risk regime confronting the households. If the households are risk neutral, then irrespective of the way in which the risk regime is modelled, risk does not influence their decision-making. Risk neutrality, however, is not a representative assumption about developing country farmers. The burden of evidence supports the view that farmers in general are risk averse, especially those in developing agriculture. In view of this fact, the risk regime acquires significance. Taking revenue risk to be the more appropriate measure of production risk confronting farmers (in addition to the labour market risk that they face in the casual labour

158

market), it is shown following Fabella (1989), that additive risk mimics risk neutrality in that it does not affect the optimisation conditions. Thus, an additive risk specification ends up not accounting for the presence of risk at all, since the risk parameters drop out of the first order conditions. On the other hand, multiplicative risk explicitly introduces risk factors into the optimisation conditions. For various other reasons as well it is preferable to use a multiplicative risk formulation. For one, Newbery and Stiglitz (1981) show that starting from an additive risk model one ends up with a multiplicative model in the aggregate. Further, although the use of an additive specification simplifies the subsequent estimation, it destroys the homogeneity of the production function and hence precludes the use of any duality approaches predicated on this property. Finally, the additive risk model turns out to be nested within that incorporating risk multiplicatively, and may therefore easily be tested for using the latter specification. For all these reasons, we prefer to introduce risk multiplicatively in our model.

A multiplicative risk specification, however, introduces its own problems. It makes for nonseparability between the consumption and production decisions of the households, so that the variables endogenous to the system have to be solved for simultaneously. Given the demanding data and estimation requirements of a simultaneous equations system, however, we observe that various methods have been adopted in characterising a simpler solution. After briefly reviewing these alternative strategies, we prefer to take the following course of action. Introducing risk multiplicatively into our model, we first test for separability between the production and consumption decisions. Thus, instead of *presuming* separability on the basis of one set of assumptions or another, we *test* for it empirically. We find that indeed separability holds for our sample, insofar as the demand for labour by the households does not significantly depend upon the demographic variables. Therefore, we do not need to solve for the endogenous variables in our model simultaneously. In other words, we may solve for the off-farm labour supply and the demand for labour independently of each other.

Risk Attitudes and Policy Implications

Before proceeding further let us retrace our steps a little. An important maintained hypothesis in our study has been, that developing country farmers are mostly risk averse, and certainly not risk neutral. Since this hypothesis is important to our analysis, and since every hypothesis can hardly be tested afresh, we thoroughly reviewed the available empirical evidence to try and discover if, indeed, it is tenable. Our analysis of a host of evidence relating to farmers engaged in diverse decision situations, in widely varying agroclimatic regions, and possessing differential management skills, led us to the working hypothesis that farmers are predominantly risk averse, with those in developing agriculture more so than their developed country counterparts. While we shall consider the implications of this conclusion for issues relating to rural labour markets in due course, can we say anything about the policy implications of this 'finding' *per se*?

At the practical level, what implications we can draw therefrom for policy is a somewhat vexed issue. On the one hand, Roumasset (1979) argues for the *unimportance* of incorporating risk aversion (and risk) in analyses of farmer behaviour; his argument being premised on an empirical analysis of a sample of rice farmers from the Phillipines. Walker (1981) seems to endorse his view. On the other hand, Moscardi and de Janvry (1977) argue that '[K]nowledge of attitude toward risk for particular categories of peasants ... makes it possible ... to determine packages of technological and institutional practices optimally tailored to peasants' economic behaviour'. Shahabuddin *et.al.* (1986) reiterate this view. These authors, however, don't quite indicate how this 'tailoring' may be achieved. First, estimation of individual risk preferences (or even those for groups of farmers) *on a continuing basis on any large scale* may be impractical on grounds of cost, time and effort (in addition to the nuisance cost to the subjects involved). In other words, tailoring policies to individual or group preferences, say for the twin categories of small and large farmers, may not be a practical option. Moreover, if the distribution of preferences were found to be narrowly concentrated (as claimed by Binswanger), perhaps the gains to be had from such tailoring would not be substantial enough anyway. Secondly, we found that risk attitudes are not invariant across farmers but can, in fact, be explained by certain socioeconomic factors. It appears that farmers with a smaller asset base, lower education and smaller off-farm income are relatively risk averse. This would suggest that a more feasible policy option than gearing technology to group preferences would be to design programmes to remove or mitigate these constraints. Provision of credit, marketing facilities and access to inputs (perhaps on the lines of the 'solidarity group scheme'[1] mentioned in Moscardi and de Janvry's study of Mexican agriculture) would serve to ease the asset constraint. Provision of pervasive extension services would help in making up for the low education levels. Development of nonfarm rural employment opportunities may help in hedging the uncertainties relating to on-farm production by providing alternative sources of income which are not necessarily subject to the same risks. Finally, it should be emphasized that studies estimating the gains to be had in moving from risk aversion to risk neutrality are so few, that rigid views regarding the complete unimportance of incorporating risk preferences in farm decision analysis are just not tenable.

The Sample and its Aptness

For the purpose of empirical estimation we employ ICRISAT's farm household data pertaining to a fairly large number of households tracked over the 10 year period from 1975-76 to 1984-85. The data set provides detailed household-specific information on a large number of variables of interest. The households were purposively, randomly collected to be representative of the diverse agroclimatic variations across India's semi-arid tropics. For these reasons the conclusions drawn from this study should be quite generally applicable. We find that the cultivator households possess a fairly small assets base — land and nonland. The soils are generally poor and the rainfall low and erratic. For the most part, the land is unirrigated, leaving little scope for multiple cropping. The use of chemical fertilizers and large machinery is minuscule. The households are burdened with large families considering their assets base. The formal education levels of the family members are very low, averaging not even the primary level. There appears to be significant involuntary unemployment. Thus, the sample households are characterised by a meagre and low productivity assets base, physical as well as human capital, and a rural environment fraught with high production and labour market risks. In such an environment the risk variables may be expected to assume relative importance in the context of rural household decision-making.

The Demand for Labour: Some Implications for Policy

We first estimate the demand for labour functions. To appreciate the wider context underlying this exercise, consider that in developing (as also many developed) countries the government intervenes in the agricultural sector on a regular basis in more ways than one. In studying the diverse effects and gauging the efficacy of this intervention, one must consider both the effects on production as well as consumption. Especially when the producers are themselves the largest group of consumers (of the staples), as in most of developing agriculture. Now, it is often argued that the government agricultural policies only or primarily benefit the cultivators, particularly large farmers (Mitra, 1977). The benefits of higher output prices and subsidized input prices, it is pointed out, go to the cultivators/large farmers who contribute majorly to production and marketed surplus, not landless households or the small farmers. Similarly, infrastructure improvements such as irrigation and provision of *mandis* or produce markets benefit the cultivators/large farmers. To avail of cheap credit one must have adequate collateral, of which land is the most important in rural areas. Consequently, most of the credit get cornered by the cultivators/large farmers (Hanumantha Rao, 1975). The landless, by implication, do not directly benefit from most of these measures, and the small farmers comparatively little. The former, and sometimes even the latter, are on the contrary hurt by the 'high' statutory minimum/procurement prices of staple commodities, for these commodities constitute overwhelming proportions of their expenditure (Mitra, *ibid.*). While none of these assertions need necessarily be wholly correct (see Tyagi, 1979), arguably, on the credit side of the balance sheet the most important benefit that these groups stand to derive from such government intervention is supposed to be in terms of the increased demand for hired labour that production and productivity increases entail. It is in this broader context that we consider the demand for hired labour, for almost all of it is supplied by the landless and small farmer households.

The theoretical literature shows that under reasonably plausible conditions, an increase in marginal production risk would lead to a decline in the demand for hired labour. If this effect were strong enough, it could negate or even overwhelm the positive effect of the other shifter variables. In the event an important result of our study is, that production risk does *not* have a significant negative effect on the demand for hired labour and that the corresponding elasticity is negligible. This should set to rest the concern that the increased yield variability associated with the positive agricultural price policy adopted in many developing countries (India, for instance), may have depressed the demand for hired labour. Furthermore, although the real output price has a positive effect on hired labour demand, this effect is insignificant. The associated elasticity of 0.13 falls at the lower end of the results available for other developing countries (Table 7.1), with the caveat that these latter results pertain not to hired labour *per se* but to total (i.e. family plus hired) labour demand.[2] Thus, a positive price policy, whatever its benefits in terms of production and productivity,

Table 7.1 International evidence on the demand for labour in developing agriculture

	Elasticity of the total demand for labour[a] with respect to					
Country	Output price	Wage rate	Number of workers	Number of dependents	Land	Capital
Taiwan	2.25	na[b]	na	na	na	na
Malaysia	1.61	-1.47	na	na	na	na
Thailand	1.90	na	na	na	na	na
Korea	0.57	na	na	na	0.30	na
Sierra Leone	0.14	na	na	na	na	na
Nigeria	0.12	na	na	na	0.02	na

[a] Total demand for labour = Family plus hired labour demand.
[b] 'na' denotes 'not available'. While the variable in question was included as a regressor, the study did not report the corresponding labour demand elasticity.

Source: Table 1-5 in Singh, Squire and Strauss (1986, p. 32), and original readings.

does not promise to be very effective in raising employment in the Indian semi-arid regions. But if price variables are not significant shifter variables of the demand for labour, what factors qualify for this purpose?

We find the nonprice technological variables to be comparatively important in this regard. Indeed, gross cropped area is found to be the single most important factor with an elasticity of 0.95. In view of the physical land constraint in many developing countries particularly in Asia, this points towards the importance of land-augmenting technological change. Thus, increased irrigation, fertiliser use and even machinery for certain operations enable the pushing-out of the extensive margin, lengthen the cropping period, permit the substitution of relatively labour-intensive crops, and increase the cropping intensity. All these effects, in turn, are employment enhancing. And indeed, we find that the percentage area irrigated and input expenditure variables exercise a significant positive influence on labour demand, even though the associated elasticities are modest. This primacy of nonprice factors may not generally hold true for developing agriculture, however, although not much international evidence is available on the demand for labour (leave alone hired labour) to permit any conclusions with confidence. Thus, Table 7.1 informs us that for both Korea as well as Nigeria the labour demand elasticities with respect to the land variable are modest at best, and appear to be substantially less than the (output) price elasticities.

Finally, nonland assets (which may be taken to proxy the availability of capital), is found to be the other important shifter variable with an associated elasticity of 0.24. This variable would govern how intensively the farm household is able to utilise its land base, and may hence be taken to reflect the importance of easing the credit constraints that exist.

The Market Supply of Labour: Some Implications for Policy

Magnitude of Market Labour Supply

We next examine the off-farm labour supply decisions of the cultivator households within the framework of a farm household model. Although we also study the market labour supply of landless households, using a representative consumer model, the more interesting case is the former. We extend the farm household model by including the moments of the revenue risk distribution to capture the production risks confronting cultivators. An important issue prompting this exercise was to empirically test the possibility that the cultivators use the casual labour market as a hedge against production risk. This enquiry has other significant implications as well. Thus, the agricultural commodity price stabilisation literature (Newbery and Stiglitz, 1981) discusses the impact of price stability in terms of efficiency gains/losses and the changes in revenue from on-farm production. But this ignores the fact that cultivators may also be significant operators in the casual labour market (given their small land base), so that price stabilisation (or reduced production risk) will affect the producer income from off-farm work activities as well. However, we do not pursue this line of enquiry, and it needs to be taken up separately. Another implication of the basic issue raised above is whether production risk is a significant shifter of the market labour supply curve. For if the cultivators increase their market labour supply by a large enough magnitude in response to increased production risk, this may negate partially or wholly any rightward shifts of the labour demand curve. Consequently, increased employment would materialise only at reduced real wage rates. Our results

Table 7.2 International evidence on cultivator household labour supply in developing agriculture

	Elasticity of total labour supply[a] with respect to					
Country	Output price	Wage rate	Number of workers	Number of dependents	Land	Capital
Taiwan	-1.54	0.17	1.27	0.20	-0.77	-0.06
Malaysia	-0.57	0.11	0.62	0.12	-0.41	na[b]
Thailand	-0.62	0.26	0.94	-0.28	-0.19	-0.19
Korea	-0.11	0.11	na	na	-0.08	na
Sierra Leone	-0.09	0.26	0.55	0.11	-0.01	-0.05
Sierra Leone	-4.42	17.18	14.36	3.78	-0.94	-4.90
Nigeria	-0.06	0.10	na	na	na	na

[a] Total labour supply = Own-farm plus off-farm labour supply (except in the second Sierra Leone sample where the elasticities refers to off-farm labour supply only).

[b] 'na' denotes 'not available'. While the variable in question was included as a regressor, the study did not report the corresponding labour supply elasticity.

Source: Table 1A-4 in Singh, Squire and Strauss (1986, p. 46), and original readings.

show that production risk has a significant *negative* effect on the magnitude of hiring-out by cultivator households. In other words, the cultivators are unable to use the casual labour market to hedge the production risk that they encounter. The reason for this is probably that depressed production conditions also depress the labour market opportunities (even though this relation may not be statistically significant *per se*). This result also implies that the increased yield variability associated with the positive price policies used as instruments in developing and developed countries does not cause the market labour supply curve to shift rightwards. In fact, if anything, it causes the labour supply curve to shift leftwards.

The real output price has a negative effect on cultivator household labour supply with an associated elasticity of -0.23, although this effect is statistically insignificant. This result is in line with the evidence from other developing countries reported in Table 7.2. Thus, a positive price policy does not *per se* shift the supply of labour curve outwards.

Cultivator household labour supply is significantly positively related to the expected real wage rate, with a substantial elasticity of 0.36. This is contrary to the results of previous studies of Indian farmers which reported a significantly negative wage response (Bardhan, 1979, 1984a; Rosenzweig, 1980). Part of the explanation for this difference may lie in the possible mis-specification of the estimation model in the earlier studies. For when we use actual (and not desired) labour supply as the regressand and omit the risk terms as did the earlier studies, the wage variable turns out to have a significantly negative coefficient. Again, our result is in line with the evidence from other developing countries reported in Table 7.2. In the case of landless households we find a *negative* labour supply response to the real wage rate (which, albeit, is insignificant). This is because in representative consumer models an increase in wages would lead to an increase in the demand for consumption and leisure by raising real incomes. Consequently, labour supply would decline. In farm household models on the other hand, the rise in the real wage rate also raises the on-farm cost of production of the cultivator. As a result household income may decline in the net, causing a decrease in the demand for leisure or an increase in the supply of labour.

Gross cropped area, percentage area irrigated, input expenditure and nonland assets were generally quite important in determining labour market participation, decreasing the likelihood and/or the magnitude of labour supply by cultivator households. The elasticities associated with the magnitude of response, however, were rather modest. The evidence on other developing countries reported in Table 7.2 broadly concurs with our results.

Finally, the caste variable turns out to be fairly insignificant vis-a-vis the labour allocation decisions of cultivator households (except that it marginally discourages female labour supply from such households). The same observation holds for the demand for hired labour analysed earlier. Taken together, this is of import as it seems to indicate the primacy of economic factors over parochial sociocultural considerations with regard to matters of employment.

Decomposition of the Market Labour Supply Response

We pointed out in chapter 6 the unsuitability of the tobit model for our purposes and preferred to use the Heckman two-step procedure to derive estimates of the nonlimit response of market labour supply in response to changes in various explanatory variables. The tobit model may, however, be quite appropriate for other purposes — specifically, for decomposing the total labour supply response into changes in the probability of being above the limit (i.e. of labour market participation) and the magnitude of the nonlimit response (i.e. the number of days of labour supply). Thus, if the labour supply increases in response to a decrease in the output price, how will this increase be apportioned between a marginal increase in the number of days worked and an increase in the probability of working any days at all?

McDonald and Moffitt (1980) show that the total change in the dependent variable y on account of a change in the ith variable in the set of regressors X, may be decomposed as follows:

$$\frac{\partial E(y)}{\partial X_i} = \Phi(z) \frac{\partial E(y^*)}{\partial X_i} + E(y^*) \frac{\partial \Phi(z)}{\partial X_i} \tag{7.1}$$

where y^* are the nonlimit observations on the dependent variable so that $E(y^*) = X\beta + \sigma\phi/\Phi$, and z (= $X\beta/\sigma$) is a standard normal variate. Therefore, the total change in y may be dichotomized into: (i) the change in y of the observations above the limit weighted by the probability of being above the limit, and (ii) the change in the probability of being above the limit weighted by the expected value of the nonlimit observations on y. Furthermore, we have

$$\frac{\partial E(y^*)}{\partial X_i} = \beta_i \left[1 - z \frac{\phi(z)}{\Phi(z)} - \frac{\phi^2(z)}{\Phi^2(z)} \right] \tag{7.2}$$

$$\frac{\partial \Phi(z)}{\partial X_i} = \phi(z) \frac{\beta_i}{\sigma} \tag{7.3}$$

Substituting (7.2) and (7.3) into (7.1) it can be shown that:

$$\frac{\partial E(y)}{\partial X_i} = \Phi(z) \beta_i \tag{7.4}$$

Dividing (7.1) throughout by $\Phi(z)\beta_i$, the fraction of the total effect attributable to the nonlimit response is equal to $[1 - z\phi(z)/\Phi(z) - \phi^2(z)/\Phi^2(z)]$. Estimating z at the mean levels of the regressors, we find this fraction to be 0.441 for the cultivator households. In other words, following a change in the regressors only about 44% of the change in off-farm labour supply by cultivator households will be due to the nonlimit response i.e. due to a change in the number of days worked.

About 56% will be due to a change in the probability of being in the labour force. This sounds plausible, because as Walker and Ryan (1990) point out, men are preferred for self-cultivation in our sample villages and women for off-farm labour. Therefore, an increase in labour supply by the household occurs more on account of an increased participation rate by women (translating into an increased probability of labour supply by the household), than by those already in the labour market working more. This comes out even more clearly when we carry out the decomposition for (cultivator household) female labour alone. Thus, the fraction of the nonlimit response works out to only 0.325, indicating an overwhelming change in the participation rate of women and hence in the probability of female labour supply. By contrast, for landless households, this fraction works out to 0.728. That is, almost three-fourths of the total response on account of a change in the regressors is manifested in a change in the magnitude of the nonlimit response, namely the number of days worked off-farm by those already in the labour force. Only one-fourth of the change in on account of an increased participation rate by the other family members. Evidently, the economic and policy implications of a policy initiative will be of significantly different importance for cultivator households than for landless households, and for females than for males.

Process of Rural Wage Determination

The process of rural wage determination was not the area of focus in this monograph. Therefore, we do not undertake an examination of the alternative theories of rural wage determination. Some brief comments may be offered, however. In view of the fact that our context has been the *daily* casual labour market in the semi-arid tracts of south-central India, efficiency wage theories and implicit contract theories are probably irrelevant as plausible explanations of wage determination. Such theories would make more sense in situations involving contracts substantially longer than a day (Rosenzweig, 1988). The theory of interlinked markets is inconsistent with our sample as the proportion of farmers reporting interlinked contracts was very small and most of these contracts were confined to the permanent or tied labour in these regions (Jodha, 1984; Binswanger *et.al.*, 1984; Walker and Ryan, 1990). It is the fourth category of theories — the subsistence wage theories — on which our empirical evidence sheds some light. Subsistence wage theories hypothesize that wages are determined by exogenous factors such as sociocultural, biological and moral norms. By implication, changes in labour market conditions do not have any effect on the wage rate. Our evidence does not support this assertion. We find the real output price to be the single most important variable in the determination of cultivator household wage rates. A closer examination reveals, however, that this is true only for the female workers from cultivator households, and not for the male workers. This again reflects Walker and Ryan's (*ibid.*) observation that males were preferred for self-cultivation and females for off-farm labour supply. Understandably, then, female wage rates would be more responsive to changes in labour market conditions. Depending on the labour group, several other variables are found to be important as well. Thus, wage rates are significantly responsive to personal characteristics, human capital variables and technological factors, and hence our evidence does not vindicate the subsistence theories of wage determination.

Disequilibrium in the Casual Labour Market

The partial analyses of the demand and supply of wage labour are supplemented by a simultaneous equations analysis of the rural labour market. Given non-clearing rural labour markets in developing agriculture, a disequilibrium model is constructed and estimated. The estimation results are qualitatively more or less in consonance with those obtained from the partial analyses, and the differences are rather few. In addition, the disequilibrium model yields some results that are not obtainable from the partial analyses. Thus, we are able to *test* the hypothesis that the casual labour market does not clear. We are also able to test the hypothesis that rural wages have a tendency to be sticky in the downward direction. The results reveal that most of the sample period was characterised by excess supply or equilibrium in the daily, casual labour market in our study regions. We also find that the speed of wage adjustment in the upward direction significantly exceeds that in the downward direction, supporting the hypothesis that rural wages in developing agriculture tend to be sticky in the downward direction. While these results are in agreement with the stylized facts regarding developing agriculture, particularly Asian agriculture, some caveats must be entered. For estimating the model we had to make do with only a small number of observations (just 27), which leaves us with rather few degrees of freedom. Furthermore, aggregation further reduced the already small variation exhibited by some of the explanatory variables, coercing us to omit some of these from the simultaneous equations regression analysis. Both these factors would make for relatively large sampling variances of the estimators. For these reasons, although the disequilibrium model results are quite good, we repose greater confidence in the results from the partial analyses and prefer to retain the conclusions drawn from them.

Notes

1   A 'solidarity group' comprised five to twenty members where each member could avail of certain institutionally provided services as long as atleast one member of the group had legal title to his or her land.
2   The international evidence presented in Tables 7.1 and 7.2 comes from studies estimating 'fully specified models'. Since they did not use regression analysis we cannot talk in terms of the elasticity estimates presented in these studies being 'significant' or otherwise. Hence the comparison between our results and the results in these studies can only be in terms of orders of magnitude.

Bibliography

Adulavidhaya, K. *et.al.* (1984), 'The Comparative Statics of the Behaviour of Agricultural Households in Thailand', *Singapore Economic Review*, vol. 29, no. 1, pp. 69-76.

Agarwal, B. (1990), 'Social Security and the Family in Rural India: Coping with Seasonality and Calamity', *Journal of Peasant Studies*, vol. 17, no. 3, pp. 341-412.

Ahmed, I. (1980), 'Technological Change, Agrarian Structure and Labour Absorption in Bangladesh Rice Cultivation' in *ILO-ARTEP (1980)*.

Amemiya, T. (1974), 'Bivariate Probit Analysis: Minimum Chi-square Methods', *Journal of the American Statistical Association*, vol. 69, no. 348, pp. 940-944.

Amemiya, T. (1985), *Advanced Econometrics*, Harvard University Press, Cambridge, Massachusetts.

Antle, J. M. (1987), 'Econometric Estimation of Producers' Risk Attitudes', *American Journal Of Agricultural Economics*, vol. 69, no. 3, pp. 509--522.

Antle, J. M. (1989), 'Nonstructural Risk Attitude Estimation', *American Journal Of Agricultural Economics*, vol. 71, no. 3, pp. 774-784.

Bardhan, K. (1977), 'Rural Employment, Wages and Labour Markets in India: A Survey of Research II', *Economic and Political Weekly*, vol. 12, no. 27, pp. 1062-1074.

Bardhan, P. (1973), 'Size, Productivity and Returns to Scale: An Analysis of Farm-level Data in Indian Agriculture', *Journal of Political Economy*, vol. 81, no. 6, pp. 1370-1386.

Bardhan, P. (1978), 'On Labour Absorption in South Asian Rice Agriculture with particular reference to India' in *Bardhan et.al. (1978)*.

Bardhan, P. *et.al.* (1978), *Labour Absorption in Indian Agriculture: Some Exploratory Investigations*, International Labour Office, Bangkok.

Bardhan, P. (1979a), 'Labour Supply functions in a Poor Agrarian Economy', *American Economic Review*, vol. 69, no. 1, pp. 73-83.

Bardhan, P. (1979b), 'Wages and Unemployment in a Poor Agrarian Economy: A Theoretical and Empirical Analysis', *Journal of Political Economy*, vol. 87, no. 3, pp. 479-500.

Bardhan, P. (1983), 'Labour-Tying in a Poor Agrarian Economy: A Theoretical and Empirical Analysis', *Quarterly Journal of Economics*, vol. 48, no. 3, pp. 501-514.

Bardhan, P. (1984a), *Land, Labour and Rural Poverty*, Oxford University Press, Delhi.

Bardhan, P. (1984b) 'Determinants of Supply and Demand for Labour in a Poor Agrarian Economy: An Analysis of Household Survey Data from Rural West Bengal' in *Binswanger and Rosenzweig (eds.) (1984)*.

Bardsley, P. and M. Harris (1987), 'An Approach to the Econometric Estimation of Attitudes to Risk in Agriculture', *Australian Journal Of Agricultural Economics*, vol. 36, no. 1, pp. 112-126.

Barnum, H.N. and L. Squire (1979), 'An Econometric Application of the Theory of the Farm Household', *Journal of Development Economics*, vol. 6, no. 1, pp. 79-102.

Batra, R.N. and A. Ullah (1974), 'Competitive Firm and the Theory of Input Demand Under Price Uncertainty', *Journal of Political Economy*, vol. 82, no. 3, pp. 537-548.

Battese, G.E., T.J. Coelli and T.C. Colby (1989), 'Estimation of Frontier Production Functions and the efficiencies of Indian farms using panel data from ICRISAT's village level studies', *Journal of Quantitative Economics*, vol. 5, no. 2, pp. 327-348.

Benjamin, D. (1992), 'Household Composition, Labour Markets and Labour Demand: Testing for Separation in Agricultural Household Models', *Econometrica*, vol. 60, no. 2, pp. 287-322.

Berry, R.A. and W.R. Cline (1979), *Agrarian Structure and Productivity in Developing Countries*, Johns Hopkins University Press, Baltimore.

Bessler, D. (1979), 'Risk Management and Risk Preferences in Agriculture: Discussion', *American Journal of Agricultural Economics*, vol. 61, no. 5, pp. 1078-1080.

Bhalla, S. (1979), 'Farm Size, Productivity and Technical Change in Indian Agriculture' in *Berry and Cline (1979)*.

Binswanger, H.P. (1978a), 'Risk Attitudes of Rural Households in Semi-Arid Tropical India', *Economic and Political Weekly*, vol. 13, no. 25, pp. A49-A62.

Binswanger, H.P. (1978b), *The Economics of Tractors in South Asia: An Analytical Eeview*, Agricultural Development Council, New York and International Crops Research Institute for the Semi-Arid Tropics, Hyderabad, India.

Binswanger, H.P. (1980), 'Attitudes toward Risk: Experimental

Measurement in Rural India', *American Journal of Agricultural Economics*, vol. 62, no. 3, pp. 395-407.

Binswanger, H.P. (1981), 'Attitudes toward Risk: Theoretical Implications of an Experiment in Rural India', *Economic Journal*, vol. 91, no. 365, pp. 867-890.

Binswanger, H.P. *et.al.* (1984), 'Common Features and Contrasts in Labor Relations in the Semiarid Tropics of India' in *Binswanger and Rosenzweig (1984)*.

Binswanger, H.P. and M.R. Rosenzweig (eds.) (1984), *Contractual Arrangements, Employment and Wages in Rural Labour Markets in Asia*, Yale University Press, New Haven.

Binswanger, H.P. and D.A. Sillers (1983), 'Risk Aversion and Credit Constraints in Farmers' Decision-Making: A Reinterpretation', *Journal of Development Studies*, vol. 20, no. 1, pp. 5-21.

Block, M. and J. Heineke (1973), 'The Allocation of Effort under Uncertainty: The Case of Risk Averse Behaviour', *Journal of Political Economy*, vol. 81, no. 2, pp. 376-385.

Boan, J.A. (1955), 'A Study of Farmers' Reaction to Uncertain Price Expectations', *Journal of Farm Economics*, vol. 37, no. 1, pp. 90-95.

Bond, G and B. Wonder (1980), 'Risk Attitudes Amongst Australian Farmers', *Australian Journal of Agricultural Economics*, vol. 24, no. 1, pp. 16-34.

Bramlett, G.A. and P.R. Johnson (1959), *Reducing Market Risks in Selling Selected Farm Products*, Unpublished.

Brink, L. and B. McCarl (1978), 'The Tradeoff between Expected Return and Risk among Cornbelt Farmers', *American Journal of Agricultural Economics*, vol. 60, no. 2, pp. 259-263.

Brownlee, O.H. and W. Gainer (1949), 'Farmers' Price Anticipation and the Role of Uncertainty in Farm Planning', *Journal of Farm Economics*, vol. 31, no. 2, pp. 266-275.

Charemza, W.W. and D. Deadman (1992), *New Directions in Econometric Practice*, Edward Elgar, England.

Conklin, F., A. Baquet and A. Halter (1977), *A Bayesian Simulation Approach for Estimating Value of Information: An Application to Frost Forecasting*, Oregon State University Agricultural Experiment Station Technical Bulletin No. 136.

Dandekar, V. M. (1980), 'Introduction', *Indian Journal Of Agricultural Economics*, vol. 35, no. 2, pp. 1-12.

Dardanoni, V. (1988), 'Optimal Choices Under Uncertainty: The Case of

Two-argument Utility Functions', *Economic Journal*, vol. 98, no. 391, pp. 429-450.

Da Vanzo, J., D. de Tray and D. Greenberg (1976), 'The Sensitivity of Male Labour Supply Estimates to the Choice of Assumptions', *Review of Economics and Statistics*, vol. 58, no. 3, pp. 313-325.

Davidson, J.R. and R.L. Mighell (1963), 'Tracing Farmers' Reactions to Uncertainties', *Journal of Farm Economics*, vol. 45, no. 3, pp. 577-86.

Deaton, A. and J. Muellbauer (1980), *Economics and Consumer Behaviour*, Cambridge University Press, Cambridge, Massachusetts.

Deolalikar, A.B. and W.P.M. Vijverberg (1983), 'The heterogeneity of family and hired labour in agricultural production: A test using district level data from India', *Journal of Development Economics*, vol. 8, no. 2, pp. 45-69.

Dickey, D.A. and W.A. Fuller (1979), 'Distributions of the estimators for autoregressive time series with a unit root', *Journal of the American Statistical Association*, vol. 74, no. 366, pp. 427-431.

Dickey, D.A. and W.A. Fuller (1981), 'Likelihood Ratio Statistics for Autoregressive Time Series with a Unit Root, *Econometrica*, vol. 49, no. 4, pp. 1057-1072.

Dillon, J.L. and P.L. Scandizzo (1978), 'Risk Attitudes of Subsistence Farmers in Northeast Brazil: A Sampling Approach', *American Journal of Agricultural Economics*, vol. 69, no. 3, pp. 425-435.

Dreze, Jean and A. Mukherjee (1989), 'Labour Contracts in Rural India: Theories and Evidence' in Sukhomoy Chakravarty (ed.) *The Balance between Industry and Agriculture in Economic Development, vol. 3: Manpower and Transfers*, The Macmillan Press, London.

Dreze, J. and A. Sen (1995), *India: Economic Development and Social Opportunity*, Oxford University Press, Delhi.

Eswaran, M. and A. Kotwal (1985), 'A Theory of Two-tier Labour Markets in Agrarian Economies', *American Economic Review*, vol. 75, no. 1, pp. 162-177.

Engle, R.F. and C. Granger (1987), 'Cointegration and Error Correction: Representation, Estimation and Testing', *Econometrica*, vol. 55, no. 2, pp. 251-276.

Evenson, R.E. and H.P. Binswanger (1984), 'Estimating Labour Demand Functions for Indian Agriculture' in *Binswanger and Rosenzweig (1984)*.

Fabella, R.V. (1989), 'Separability and Risk in the Static Household Production Model', *Southern Economic Journal*, vol. 55, no. 4, pp.

954-961.

Fackler, P.L. (1991), 'Modeling Interdependence: An Approach to Simulation and Elicitation', *American Journal of Agricultural Economics*, vol. 73, no. 4, pp. 1091-1097.

Fafchamps, M. (1989), *Sequential Decisions Under Uncertainty and Labour Market Failure: a model of household behaviour in the African Semi-Arid Tropics*, Ph.D dissertation, University of California, Berkeley.

Fafchamps, M. (1993), 'Sequential Labour Decisions Under Uncertainty: An Estimable Household Model of West-African Farmers', *Econometrica*, vol. 61, no. 5, pp. 1173-97.

Fair, R.C. and D.M. Jaffee (1972), 'Methods of Estimation for Markets in Disequilibrium', *Econometrica*, vol. 40, no. 3, pp. 497-514.

Feder, G., R. Just and D. Zilberman (1985), 'Adoption of Agricultural Innovations in Developing Countries', *Economic Development and Cultural Change*, vol. 33, no. 2, pp. 355-398.

Fishburn, P.C. (1967), 'Methods of Estimating Additive Utilities', *Management Science*, vol. 13 (Series A), pp. 435-453.

Francisco, E. and J. Anderson (1972), 'Chance and Choice West of the Darling', *Australian Journal of Agricultural Economics*, vol. 16, no. 1, pp. 82-93.

Granger, C.W.J. (1969), 'Investigating causal relations by econometric models and cross-spectral methods', *Econometrica*, vol. 37, no. 1, pp. 24-36.

Granger, C.W.J. (1981), 'Some Properties of Time Series Data and their Use in Econometric Model Specifications', *Journal of Econometrics*, vol. 16, no. 1, pp. 121-130.

Grisley, W. and E.D. Kellogg (1987), 'Risk-Taking Preferences of Farmers in northern Thailand: Measurement and Implications', *Agricultural Economics*, vol. 1, no. 1, pp. 127-142.

Guilkey, D. and M. Salemi (1982), 'Small Sample Properties of Three Tests of Granger Causal Orderings in a Bivariate Stochastic System', *Review of Economics and Statistics*, vol. 64, no. 4, pp. 668-680.

Halter, A.N. and C. Beringer (1960), 'Cardinal Utility Functions and Managerial Behaviour', *Journal of Farm Economics*, vol. 42, no. 1, pp. 118-132.

Halter, A.N. and R. Mason (1978), 'Utility Measurement for Those Who Need to Know', *Western Journal of Agricultural Economics*, vol. 3, no. 2, pp. 99-109.

Ham, J. (1982), 'Estimation of a Labour Supply Model with Constraints due to Unemployment and Underemployment', *Review of Economic Studies*, vol. 49, no. 3, pp. 335-354.

Hanumantha Rao, C.H. (1975), *Technological Change and Distribution of Gains in Indian Agriculture*, Macmillan, Delhi.

Hanumantha Rao, C.H., S.K. Ray and K. Subbarao (1988), *Unstable Agriculture and Droughts: Implications for Policy*, Vikas, New Delhi.

Hazell, P.B.R. (1982), 'Application of Risk Preference Estimates in Firm-Household and Agricultural Sector Models', *American Journal of Agricultural Economics*, vol. 64, no. 2, pp. 384-390.

Heckman, J.J. (1979), 'Sample Selection Bias as a Specification Error', *Econometrica*, vol. 47, no. 1, pp. 153-161.

Hsiao, C. (1979), 'Autoregressive Modelling of Canadian Money and Income Data', *Journal of the American Statistical Association*, vol. 74, no. 367, pp. 553-560.

Huffman, W. (1980), 'Farm and Off-Farm Work Decisions: The Role Of Human Capital', *Review of Economics and Statistics*, vol. 62, no. 1, pp. 14-23.

ILO-ARTEP (1980), *Employment Expansion in Asian Agriculture: A Comparative Analysis of South Asian Countries*, International Labour Office, Bangkok.

Ishikawa, S. (1978), *Labour Absorption in Asian Agriculture: An Issues Paper*, International Labour Office, Bangkok.

Jodha, N.S. (1984), 'Agricultural Tenancy in Semiarid Tropical India', in *Binswanger and Rosenzweig (eds.) (1984)*.

Johnson, P.R. (1962), 'Do Farmers Hold a Preference for Risk?', *Journal of Farm Economics*, vol. 44, no. 1, pp. 200-207.

Judge, G. *et.al.* (1988), *Introduction to the Theory and Practice of Econometrics*, John Wiley, New York.

Just, R.E and R.D. Pope (1978), 'Stochastic Specification of Production Functions and Economic Implications', *Journal of Econometrics*, vol. 7, no. 1, pp. 67-86.

Juster, F.T. (1972), 'Microdata Requirements and Public Policy Designs', *Annals of Economic and Social Measurement*, vol. 1, no. 1, pp. 7-16.

Kahneman, D and A. Tversky (1979), 'prospect Theory: An Analysis of Decision Under Risk', *Econometrica*. vol. 47, no. 2, pp. 263-292.

Kalirajan, K. and R.T. Shand (1982), 'Labour Absorption in Tamil Nadu agriculture: A micro analysis', *Developing Economies*, vol. 20, no. 3, pp. 333-343.

Kanwar, S. (1991), *The Analytics of Off-Farm Labour Supply Under Alternative Risk Regimes*, Ph.D dissertation, University of California at Berkeley.

Kanwar, S. (1994), *Are Production Risk and Labour Market Risk Covariant?*, CDE Working Paper No. 24, Delhi School of Economics, University of Delhi, Delhi.

Kanwar, S. (1995), 'Do Farm Households use the Labour Market as a hedge against Revenue Risk? Evidence from Female Labour Supply', *Indian Journal of Agricultural Economics*, vol. 50, no. 4, pp. 660-667.

Kanwar, S. (1996), *Are Peasants Risk Averse? A Critical Assessment*, mimeo, Delhi School of Economics, Delhi.

Kanwar, S. (1996), *The Demand for Labour in Risky Agriculture*, CDE Working Paper No. 37, Delhi School of Economics, Delhi.

Kanwar, S. (1998), 'Are Production Risk and Labour Market Risk Covariant?', *Journal of International Development*, vol. 10, no. 1, pp. 129-146.

Kanwar, S. (1998), 'Does Risk Matter? The Case of Wage-Labour Allocation by Owner-Cultivators, *Applied Economics*, forthcoming.

Kanwar, S. (1998), 'Wage Responsiveness of Labour Supply and Demand in Nonclearing Rural Markets: The Case of Indian Agriculture', *Economics Letters*, forthcoming.

King, R.P. and L.J. Robison (1981), 'An Interval Approach to Measuring Decision Maker Preferences', *American Journal of Agricultural Economics*, vol. 63, no. 3, pp. 510-520.

Kmenta, J. (1986), *Elements of Econometrics*, The Macmillan Press, New York.

Laffont, J.J. and R. Garcia (1977), 'Disequilibrium Econometrics for Business Loans', *Econometrica*, vol. 45, no. 5, pp. 1187-1204.

Lau, L, W. Lin and P. Yotopoulos (1978), 'The Linear Logarithmic Expenditure System: An Application to Consumption Leisure Choice', *Econometrica*, vol. 46, no. 4, pp. 843-868.

Lin, W and H. Chang (1978), 'Specification of Bernoullian Utility Functions in Decision Analysis', *Agricultural Economics Research*, vol. 30, no. 1, pp. 30-36.

Lin, W., G. Dean and C. Moore (1974), 'An Empirical Test of Utility vs. Profit Maximisation in Agricultural Production', *American Journal of Agricultural Economics*, vol. 56, no. 3, pp. 497-508.

Lin, T.F. and P. Schmidt (1984), 'A Test of the Tobit Specification Against an Alternative suggested by Cragg', *Review of Economics and*

Statistics, vol. 66, no. 1, pp. 174-177.

Lipton, M. and R. Longhurst (1989), *New Seeds and Poor People*, Unwin Hyman, London.

Machina, M.J. (1989), 'Dynamic Consistency and Non-Expected Utility Models of Choice Under Uncertainty', *Journal of Economic Literature*, vol. 27, no. 4, pp. 1622-1668.

McCarthy, W. and J. Anderson (1966), 'Applied Aspects of Farmer Decision Making' in *Conference Proceedings of the Committee on Economics of Range Use and Development*, Western Agricultural Economics Research Council Report No. 8, San Francisco.

McDonald, J. and R. Moffitt (1980), 'The Uses of Tobit Analysis', *Review of Economics and Statistics*', vol. 62, no. 2, pp. 318-321.

Menezes, C, G. Geiss and J. Tressler (1980), 'Increasing Downside Risk', *American Economic Review*, vol. 70, no. 5, pp. 921-932.

Menezes, C.F. and D.L. Hanson (1970), 'On the Theory of Risk Aversion', *International Economic Review*, vol. 11, no. 3, pp. 481-487.

Mitra, A. (1977), *Terms of Trade and Class Relations*, Frank Cass, London.

Morrison, T.C. and G.G. Judge (1955), 'Impact of Price Expectation and Uncertainties on Decision Making by Poultry Firms', *Journal of Farm Economics*, vol. 37, no. 4, pp. 652-663.

Moscardi, E and A. de Janvry 1977 'Attitudes Towards Risk among Peasants: An Econometric Approach', *American Journal Of Agricultural Economics*, vol. 59, no. 4, pp. 710-716.

Naseem, S.M. (1980), 'Regional Variation and Structural Changes: Their Effects on Labour Absorption in Pakistan's Agriculture' in *ILO-ARTEP (1980)*.

Nelson, C.R. and W. Schwert (1982), 'Tests for Predictive Relationships between Time Series Variables: A Monte Carlo Investigation', *Journal of the American Statistical Association*, vol. 77, no. 377, pp. 11-18.

Newbery, D and J. Stiglitz 1981 *The Theory of Commodity Price Stabilization: A Study In The Economics of Risk*, Clarendon Press, Oxford.

Oberoi, A.S. and I. Ahmed, (1981), 'Labour Use in Dynamic Agriculture: Evidence from Punjab', *Economic and Political Weekly*, vol. 16. no. 13, pp. A2-A4.

Officer, R. and A. Halter (1968), 'Utility Analysis in a Practical Setting', *American Journal of Agricultural Economics*, vol. 50, no. 2, pp. 257-277.

Pal, S. (1996), 'Casual and Regular Contracts: Workers' Self-selection in the Rural Labour Markets in India', *Journal of Development Studies*, vol. 33, no. 1, pp. 99-116.

Parliament, C. (1984), *'Agricultural Production Cooperatives: Factors Affecting Performance'*, Ph.D dissertation, University of California, Berkeley.

Phillips, P.C.B. (1987), 'Time Series Regression with a Unit Root', *Econometrica*, vol. 55, no. 2, pp. 277-301.

Pollak, R. and T. Wales (1981), 'Demographic Variables in Demand Analysis', *Econometrica*, vol. 49, no. 6, pp. 1533-1551.

Pope, R.D. and R. Kramer (1979), 'Production Uncertainty and Factor Demands for the Competitive Firm', *Southern Economic Journal*, vol. 46, no. 2, pp. 489-501.

Pratt, J.W. (1964), 'Risk Aversion in the small and the Large', *Econometrica*, vol. 32, no. 1, pp. 122-136.

Richards, A. (1979), 'The Political Economy of Gutswirtschaft: A Comparative Analysis of East Elbian Germany, Egypt and Chile', *Comparative Studies in Society and History*, vol 21, no 4, pp. 483-518.

Robison, L.J. (1982), 'An Appraisal of Expected Utility Hypothesis Tests constructed from Responses to Hypothetical Questions and Experimental Choices', *American Journal of Agricultural Economics*, vol. 64, no. 2, pp. 367-375.

Roe, T. and T. Graham-Tomasi (1986), 'Yield Risk in a Dynamic Model of the Agricultural Household' in *I. Singh, L. Squire and J. Strauss (eds.) (1986)*.

Rosenzweig, M.R. (1980), 'Neoclassical Theory and the Optimizing Peasant: An Econometric Analysis of Market Family Labour Supply in Developing Countries', *Quarterly Journal of Economics*, vol. 94, no. 1, pp. 31-56.

Rosenzweig, M.R. (1988), 'Labour Markets in Low-Income Countries' in H. Chenery and T. N. Srinivasan (eds.) *Handbook of Development Economics*, vol. I, North-Holland, Amsterdam.

Roumasset, J. (1979), 'Unimportance of Risk for Technology Design and Agricultural Development Policy' in A. Valdes, G. Scobie and J. Dillon (eds.) *Economics and the Design of Small Farmer Technology*, Iowa State University Press, Ames, Iowa.

Rudra, A. (1982), *Indian Agricultural Economics: Myths and Realities*, Allied Publishers, New Delhi.

Sandmo, A. (1971), 'On the Theory of the Competitive Firm Under Price Uncertainty', *American Economic Review*, vol. 61, no. 1, pp. 65-73.

Sargent, T.J. (1976), 'A classical macroeconomic model for the United States', *Journal of Political Economy*, vol. 84, no. 2, pp. 207-238.

Savin, N.E. and K.J. White (1977), 'The Durbin-Watson Test for Autocorrelation with Extreme Sample Sizes or Many Regressors', *Econometrica*, vol. 45, no. 6, pp. 1989-1996.

Schoemaker, P.J.H. (1982), 'The expected utility model: its variants, purposes, evidence and limitations, *Journal of Economic Literature*, vol. 20, no. 2, pp. 529-563.

Shaban, R. (1985), 'Testing between Competing Models of Sharecropping', *Journal of Political Economy*, vol. 95, no. 5, pp. 893-920.

Shahabuddin, Q, S. Mestelman and D. Feeney (1986), 'Peasnat Behaviour Towards Risk and Socio-economic and Structural Characteristics of Farm Househoolds in Bangladesh', *Oxford Economic Papers*, vol. 38, no. 1, pp. 122-130.

Singh, I. and S. Janakiram (1986), 'Agricultural Household Modeling in a Multicrop Environment: Case Studies in Korea and Nigeria' in *Singh, Squire and Strauss (eds.)*.

Singh, I, L. Squire and J. Strauss (eds.) (1986) *Agricultural Household Models: Extensions, Applications and Policy*, The Johns Hopkins University Press, Baltimore.

Singh, I, L. Squire and J. Strauss (1986), 'The Basic Model: Theory, Empirical Results and Policy Conclusions' in *Singh, Squire and Strauss (eds.) (1986)*.

Singh, N. (1989), 'Theories of Sharecropping' in P. Bardhan (ed.) *The Economic Theory of Agrarian Institutions*, Clarendon Press, Oxford.

Singh, R.P. *et.al.* (1985), *Manual Of Instructions For Economic Investigators In ICRISAT's Village Level Studies (Revised)*, International Crops Research Institute for the Semi-Arid Tropics, Andhra Pradesh, India.

Skoufias, E. (1993), 'Labour Market Opportunities and Intrafamily time allocation in rural households in South Asia', *Journal of Development Economics*, vol. 40, no. 2, pp. 277-310.

Strauss, J. (1986), 'Estimating the Determinants of Food Consumption and Caloric Availability in rural Sierra Leone' in *Singh, Squire and Strauss (eds.) (1986)*.

Sumner, D. (1982), 'The Off-Farm Labour Supply of Farmers', *American Journal of Agricultural Economics*, vol. 64, no. 3, pp. 499-509.

Tversky, A. (1967), 'Additivity, Utility and Subjective Probability', *Journal of Mathematical Psychology*, vol. 4 (June), pp. 175-201.

Tyagi, D.S. (1979), 'Farm Prices and Class Bias in India', *Economic and Political Weekly*, vol. 14, no. 39, pp. A111-A124.

Vaidyanathan, A. (1978), 'Labour Use in Indian Agriculture: An Analysis based on Farm Management Survey Data' in *Bardhan et.al [1978]*.

Vaidyanathan, A. (1980), 'Labour Absorption in Asian agriculture: some highlights of the discussions at previous seminars' in *ILO-ARTEP (1980)*.

Wales, T. and A. Woodland (1976), 'Estimation of Household Utility Functions and Labour Supply Response', *International Economic Review*, vol. 17, no. 2, pp. 397-410.

Wales, T. and A. Woodland (1977), 'Estimation of the Allocation of Time for Work, Leisure and Housework', *Econometrica*, vol. 45, no. 1, pp. 115-132.

Walker, T.S. (1981), 'Risk and adoption of hybrid maize in El Salvador', *Food Research Institute Studies*, vol. 18, no. 1, pp. 59-88.

Walker, T.S. and J.G. Ryan (1990) *Village and Household Economies in India's Semi-Arid Tropics*, Johns Hopkins Press, Baltimore.

Walker, T. and K.V. Subba Rao (1982), *Yield and Net Return Distributions in Common Village Cropping Systems in the Semi-Arid Tropics of India*, Report 41, ICRISAT.

Webster, J. and J. Kennedy (1975), 'Measuring Farmers' Tradeoffs between Expected Income and Focus Loss Income', *American Journal of Agricultural Economics*, vol. 57, no. 1, pp. 97-105.

White, K.J. (1993), *Shazam User's Referemce Manual*, McGraw-Hill.

Wickramasekara, P. (1980), 'Labour Absorption in Paddy Cultivation in Sri Lanka' in *ILO-ARTEP (1980)*.

Williams, D. (1951) 'Price Expectation and Reaction to Uncertainty by Farmers in Illinois', *Journal of Farm Economics*, vol. 33, no. 1, pp. 20-30.

Wilson, P.N. and V.R. Eidman (1983), 'An Empirical Test of the Interval approach for Estimating Risk Preferences', *Western Journal of Agricultural Economics*, vol. 8, no. 2, pp. 170-182.

Young, D.L. (1979), 'Risk Preferences of Agricultural Producers: Their Use in Extension and Research', *American Journal of Agricultural Economics*, vol. 61, no. 5, pp. 1063-1079.

Zeckhauser, R. and E. Keeler (1970), 'Another Type of Risk Aversion', *Econometrica*, vol. 38, no. 5, pp. 661-665.

Index

References from Notes are indicated by 'n' after the page reference